THE
IRISH COUNTRYWOMEN'S ASSOCIATION
BOOK OF TEA AND COMPANY

ABOUT THE ICA

Founded in May 1910, the aim of the Irish Countrywomen's Association (ICA) was 'to improve the standard of life in rural Ireland through education and co-operative effort'. Today the ICA has 700 local Guilds in cities, towns and rural areas throughout Ireland. They continue to offer support and fun as well as opportunities to make friends, learn new skills and contribute to the wider community. Every day, the women share with each other nuggets of advice, tried-and-tested methods and practical help, and they hope this book will pass on some of that knowledge to you.

THE IRISH COUNTRYWOMEN'S
ASSOCIATION

Book of
Tea and
Company

Recipes and Reflections
for Every Day

General Editor Aoife Carrigy

GILL & MACMILLAN

GILL & MACMILLAN
Hume Avenue, Park West, Dublin 12
www.gillmacmillanbooks.ie

© IRISH COUNTRYWOMEN'S TRUST, **2014**
978 07171 6397 7

General Editor Aoife Carrigy
Index compiled by Eileen O'Neill
Design and print origination by Tanya M Ross, www.elementinc.ie
Illustrations by Tanya M Ross, www.elementinc.ie
Photography © Joanne Murphy, www.joanne-murphy.com
Food stylists: Carly Horan and Blondie Horan. T: 087 922 7662. W: www.styledwithlove.ie
Food cooked and baked by Carly Horan and Blondie Horan
Assistant to chefs and stylists: Katie Tsouros
Printed by Printer Trento Srl, Italy

PROPS SUPPLIED BY

Ashley Cottage Interiors, Ballyard, Tralee, Co. Kerry. T: 087 922 7662. W: www.styledwithlove.ie
Historic Interiors, Oberstown, Lusk, Co. Dublin. T: 01 843 7174
Meadows & Byrne, Dun Laoghaire, Co. Dublin. T: 01 280 4554. W: www.meadowsandbyrne.com

3 5 4 2

Contents

INTRODUCTION

Introduction by ICA National President X

A Note from the Editor XI

BUSY DAYS 1

Carrot, Cranberry & Seed Muffins 6

Toffee Apple Muffins 9

Rock Cakes 11

Queen Cakes 12

Iced Raisin Bars 15

Orange Chocolate Bars 17

Maltesers Rocky Road 19

QUIET DAYS 23

Scones with Raspberry Jam 29

Raspberry Jam 30

Iris's Idiot-proof Brown Bread 32

Wheat-free Brown Bread 33

Guinness Bread 37

Milk Rolls 39

Drop Scones 41

Battenberg Cake 45

DIFFICULT DAYS 49

Rich-in-Love Chocolate Cake 53

Chocolate Swiss Roll 57

Coffee Ring Cake 58

Flour-free Fruit Cake 60

Apple & Rhubarb Pie 62

Marmalade Shortcakes 64

Chocolate Florentines 67

PRECIOUS DAYS 71
Mother's Malt Cake Loaf 77
Nora De Buitléar's Special Occasion Dream Cake 78
Cathryn's Crazy Chocolate Bake 80
Summer Fruit Family Slice 82
Crunchy Chocolate Meringue Cake 84
Gâteau Flamand 87
Almond Tartlets 89

SUNNY DAYS 93
Dutch Rhubarb Cake 97
Courgette Cake 100
Gingerbread 103
Honey Spice Cake 104
Baked Cherry Cheesecake 109
Curd Cheesecake 110
Moist Almond Slices 111

RAINY DAYS 115
Tea Brack 121
Almond Biscuits 123
Quarkblätterteig 124
Lemon Curd 127
Lemon Cake 128
Citrus Poppy Seed Cake 131
Cheat's Passion Fruit & Lime Soufflé 133
Mango Cheesecake 134

FESTIVE DAYS 139
Orange & Cinnamon Hot Cross Buns 143
Simnel Cake 145
Almond Paste 146
Homemade Custard 147
Mid-Western Apple Cake 150
Pumpkin Pie 153

Cut-before-Christmas Cranberry Cake 155

Cranberry Mousse 157

King's Pancake 160

SIMPLER DAYS **165**

Mutton Pies 169

Spiced Damson Butter 170

Chicken Liver Pâté 172

Cauliflower, Ham & Cheese Bake 174

Salmon Mousse 177

Sardine Eggs 179

Potato Cakes 183

Leitrim Boxty 185

APPENDICES **189**

Useful Equipment & Glossary 190

Contributors 195

Acknowledgements 197

Sources 199

INDEX 201

Introduction

I am delighted to have been asked to write the introduction to *The Irish Countrywomen's Association Book of Tea and Company: Recipes and Reflections for Every Day*, which is the ICA's third book in three years with Gill & Macmillan. We have been heartened by the fantastic response to the first two books; it is so lovely to think of them both being enjoyed and consulted in many kitchens and homes across this little island of ours, and even beyond these shores.

Our third in this series of books sharing ICA wisdom and recipes, this new publication is particularly special, being the most personal of all three. We asked our members to share with us not just their favourite teatime recipes but also their personal reflections and those treasured words that they hold close to their hearts and that help them through their days.

We Irish know the importance of a cup of tea, a delicious slice of cake and a chat. We like to spend time with our friends and family, to enjoy each other's company while also enjoying a tasty treat. How many of us have had a cup of tea in our hands when an important piece of news was announced – the passing of an exam, an engagement or the imminent arrival of a new baby into our lives? And how many family or friendship issues have been unravelled and resolved over a shared cuppa?

I have always said in our house that if we could all sit down together for a chat and have a cup of tea and a nice slice of brack or a scone, we could right the wrongs of the world. This book may not be able to do that, but we hope it will inspire you to spare a few minutes of your day to think about all there is to be thankful for.

I was lucky enough to run my own baking business for a time. Like so many other ICA women before and since, I regularly baked for the local country markets and other establishments as a way of contributing to the household income. And as is true of the other contributors to this book, the recipes I share here are ones that have been tried and tested, tweaked and improved over many years of baking for family, friends and my wider community.

Life deserves to be celebrated, to be reflected on and to be punctuated by moments of pause. We hope you enjoy reading, using and dipping into this book to celebrate all of life's important moments – big and small, ordinary and extraordinary – while someone puts the kettle on!

Liz Wall
National President of the Irish Countrywomen's Association

"Find yourself a cup of tea, the teapot is behind you.
Now tell me about hundreds of things."
– *Saki*

Welcome to the third ICA book, and perhaps my favourite of all three. Like the Angelus, teatime has long been a common source of comfort here in Ireland. A cup of tea picks you up when you are down and warms you when a neighbour visits. It accompanies many a shared moment with family and consoles in times of grief and reflection.

The Irish Countrywomen's Association Book of Tea and Company: Recipes and Reflections for Every Day offers you a celebration of the humble cuppa along with a whole host of teatime recipes for treats you might serve in its company. Indeed, the notion of 'company' is central to this cookbook; being a book that celebrates the potential of words on a page as much as food on a plate, 'company' can refer to that of a loved one with whom you might share your pot of tea, or the rewards of solitude and being comfortable in your own company, or indeed the rich company offered by a book of wise words gathered together by hundreds of wise women.

What makes this book so special is the generous spirit of the contributors. These women, from all walks of life and all corners of the country, opened their beloved scrapbooks and kitchen notebooks to share their favourite recipes with the rest of us. However, they did something much braver than that too – they opened their hearts to us, and had the courage and generosity to share some of their most precious memories, most personal insights and most honest reflections.

Scattered among these recipes and reflections are lines borrowed from favourite poems, prayers, prose and philosophies, the kinds of words you might pin to your fridge door or above your desk to remind you of what's important. Like many of the recipes and, indeed, many of the women who have shared them with us, their origins might seem surprisingly diverse until you reflect on the diversity of an island that has seen so many comings and goings over the centuries. In this book there are sweet treats from France, Germany and North America, musings from Chinese philosophers and American folk singers, bons mots from history's greatest wits, and aphorisms from its greatest minds. Some of the reflections are uplifting and motivational, others are sentimental and nostalgic – all make you pause for a moment and think.

A kind and wise word, a slice of cake and a cuppa – such a combination is like a mammy's hug in a book. What's not to love about that?

Chapter 1
Busy Days

"We must be the change we wish to see in the world."
– Mahatma Gandhi

Our age-old motto in the ICA is 'Deeds not Words'. We are women accustomed to busy days, to making lists and working our way through them. We have always been practical people, unafraid to roll up our sleeves and get stuck into the business of daily life, and we have less interest in talking about doing something than we have in getting on with it.

> " People who say it cannot be done should
> not interrupt those who are doing it. "

– George Bernard Shaw

But the truth is that even the most formidably practical amongst us can sometimes allow the part of us that worries that perhaps it cannot be done after all to interrupt the part of us that is busy doing it. Sometimes it all becomes a little overwhelming, and we doubt whether our ability matches our ambition. It is at such times that we need a well-judged word to encourage us back on our way, to rally and to motivate, to reassure, and to help us keep things in perspective.

> " Have no fear of perfection–
> you'll never reach it. "

– Salvador Dalí

We don't just deserve to take the odd break from even the busiest of days; we need that momentary pause every day in order to make the best use of whatever time and energy we have at our disposal. All work and no play made Jack a dull boy, and dullness is hardly what you want to bring to getting a job done. So brighten up, put that kettle on and consider stocking up on some wholesome home baking. Not only will these treats help keep the energy up, but you will deserve their reward when reflecting on accomplishments achieved and the satisfaction of a job well done.

from In Praise of Tea

A busy day with things to do
And people I must see,
And yet somehow I find the time
For one more cup of tea.
And if the day's a dreary one
No bright or cheery news,
A biscuit and a cup of tea
Will chase away those blues.

Through happy times and troubled times,
In laughter and in tears,
We put the kettle on once more
And share the cup that cheers.

– Iris Hesselden

" You must do things you think
you cannot do. "

– Eleanor Roosevelt

" The man who moves a mountain
begins by carrying small stones. "

– Chinese proverb

Carrot, Cranberry & Seed Muffins

AN GRIANÁN, LOUTH

All sorts of seeds work well in this wholesome treat – try sunflower seeds, pumpkin seeds, sesame seeds, poppy seeds, linseed or whatever takes your fancy. And because it is a low GI recipe, you're guaranteed a slow release of energy to fuel your busy day.

Makes 12
- 2 eggs
- 100g (4oz) soft brown sugar
- 150ml (¼ pint) sunflower oil
- 150g (6oz) finely ground wholemeal flour
- 1 teaspoon baking powder
- ½ teaspoon bicarbonate of soda, sieved
- 100g/110g (4oz) raw carrot, grated
- 50g (2oz) mixed seeds, plus a little extra for topping (optional)
- 50g (2oz) dried cranberries
- 25g (1oz) sultanas

what you'll need
- 1 x 12-cup muffin tin
- 12 muffin cases
- wire rack

1. Line a muffin tin with cases. Preheat oven to 200°C/400°F/Gas 6.

2. In a food processor, whisk the eggs and sugar together until light and fluffy. Gradually pour in the oil and continue to beat.

3. Add half of the flour together with the baking powder and bicarbonate of soda and mix well before adding half of the grated carrot, half of the seeds and half of the fruit. Mix well before adding the remaining ingredients.

4. Once the ingredients are fully integrated, spoon the mixture into prepared muffin cases, sprinkle a few extra seeds on top, if desired, and bake in preheated oven for 20 minutes. Remove from the tin and allow to cool on a wire rack.

Toffee Apple Muffins

LIZ WALL, WICKLOW

Toffee apples were the highlight of many a childhood Halloween. These clever muffins recreate that evocative flavour. A nostalgic treat for any time of year.

Makes 12

- 240ml (½ pint) milk
- 100g (3½oz) butter, melted
- 85g (3oz) caster sugar
- 2 eggs, beaten
- 2 eating apples
- 300g (10oz) plain flour
- 2 teaspoons baking powder
- ½ teaspoon salt
- pinch of ground cinnamon
- 50g (2oz) toffee, broken into small pieces

what you'll need

- 12-cup muffin tin
- 12 paper cases
- wire rack

1. Preheat oven to 190°C/375°F/Gas 5. Line a muffin tin with 12 paper cases.

2. Mix together the milk, melted butter, sugar and beaten eggs.

3. Peel and chop the eating apples and set aside. Sieve the flour, baking powder, salt and cinnamon into the wet mixture. Add the chopped apple and mix thoroughly.

4. When the ingredients are fully integrated, spoon a little of the mixture into the prepared muffin cases so that each is about a quarter full. Add a few pieces of toffee to each case before topping up with the rest of the muffin mix.

5. Bake in preheated oven for 30–35 minutes until well risen and golden. Remove from the tin and allow to cool on a wire rack.

" My Mam used to say this little prayer every night:

'Please God, grant me the strength to be able to put my feet on the floor in the morning and to have the wit in my head to know that they are on it. Amen.' "

– Anna Sinnott, Wicklow

" 'Begin at the beginning,' the King said, gravely, 'and go on till you come to the end: then stop.' "

– Lewis Carroll

God,

Make me free
From fear of the future,
From anxiety of the morrow,
From bitterness towards anyone,
From cowardice in the face of danger,
From failure before opportunity,
From laziness in the face of work.
Amen.

– Author unknown

" Shoot for the moon. Even if you miss, you'll land in the stars. "

– Les Brown

Rock Cakes

BELTRA GUILD MEMBERS, SLIGO

Rock cakes sit somewhere between a scone and a bun, and are distinguished by the crispy, crunchy texture of their rocky-looking crust, which gives way to a coarse inner crumb. This traditional version is lightly spiced and sweetened with dried fruit.

Makes 12

- 225g (8oz) self-raising flour
- 1 teaspoon baking powder
- pinch of salt
- ½ teaspoon mixed spice
- 85g (3oz) margarine, lard or butter
- 85g (3oz) sugar
- 85g (3oz) currants, cleaned
- 25g (1oz) mixed peel, finely chopped
- 1 egg
- 2–3 tablespoons milk, as needed

what you'll need

- 2 baking trays or sheets
- wire rack

1. Preheat oven to 200°C/400°F/Gas 6. Prepare the baking sheets by greasing or lining with baking parchment.

2. Sieve the flour with the baking powder, salt and mixed spice. Add whatever fat you are using and rub into the flour until the mixture reaches the consistency of fine breadcrumbs. Stir in the sugar, currants and peel.

3. Beat the egg together with a tablespoon of milk and then work it into the dry ingredients until the mixture sticks together. If needed, add a little more milk to help the mixture bind, but it should be a stiff dough.

4. Use two forks to place small rocky heaps of the mixture onto the prepared baking sheets. Bake for 15–20 minutes in preheated oven until golden brown. Transfer to a wire rack for cooling before storing in an airtight container.

Queen Cakes

BELTRA GUILD MEMBERS, SLIGO

'Queen cake' is just one of the various names for this traditional recipe for what could be seen as the original cupcake. Currant buns, fairy cakes, butterfly cakes – call them what you like. They're simply delicious by any name.

Makes 12

- 110g (4oz) caster sugar
- 110g (4oz) butter, room temperature
- 2 large eggs (or 3 medium ones), beaten
- 170g (6oz) plain flour
- 85g (3oz) currants (optional)
- pinch of salt

to finish

- icing sugar, to dust or glaze

what you'll need

- 12-cup bun tin
- 12 paper cases (optional)
- wire rack

ICA Tip

You can pretty these up by slicing off the tops and cutting them in half to be popped into a dollop of whipped cream on top of each bun, making little butterfly wings.

1. Preheat oven to 200°C/400°F/Gas 6. Prepare the bun tin by greasing well or lining with paper cases.

2. Beat the butter and sugar to a smooth cream, either in a food processor or by hand in a large bowl with a wooden spoon. Add the beaten eggs little by little, thoroughly beating in each addition before adding any more. If the mixture begins to curdle when adding the egg, mix in a little of the weighed flour to bind it. The final mixture should be stiff.

3. When all the egg is added, stir in the flour, fruit and salt. Put the mixture into the well-greased bun tin or paper cases and bake for 15–20 minutes in preheated oven until golden brown.

4. Transfer to a wire rack for cooling before finishing with a light dusting of icing sugar. Or, if you prefer, you can mix the icing sugar with a little hot water to make a thick glaze to spread on top. Allow to set before serving. Store in an airtight container.

Ten Golden Rules
for Every Busy Woman

1. I am not on call to all people all of the time.

2. I have needs of my own, which may not be the same as those of my family, my colleagues or my friends.

3. I don't have to say 'yes' to every request that is made of me.

4. I don't have to carry on doing something just because I've always done it.

5. Time spent relaxing is time well spent.

6. There's no such thing as the perfect wife, perfect mother, perfect child.

7. Time spent feeling guilty could be spent doing more enjoyable things.

8. I shouldn't always do it for them if they are capable of doing it themselves.

9. I should give myself the same care and consideration that I give to others.

10. I should remember at all times, especially in the face of criticism, difficulties and anxiety, that I am doing the best I can!

– Author unknown

Iced Raisin Bars

MARY FITZGERALD, WEXFORD

My version of this recipe is adapted from a 1960s Woman's Weekly recipe that my mother used to use and that I have tweaked over the years. They make a great pick-me-up and are delicious with an afternoon cup of tea or as a lunch-box treat.

Makes 16 bars

- 110g (4oz) butter or margarine
- 110g (4oz) brown sugar (or white)
- 2 eggs, beaten
- ½ teaspoon vanilla extract
- 110g (4oz) plain flour
- 170g (6oz) raisins
- 50g (2oz) Kellogg's All-Bran or All-Bran Buds

for the glacé icing (optional)

- 160g icing sugar
- 1½ tablespoons just-boiled water

what you'll need

- 1 shallow baking tin, about 28cm x 18cm (11in x 7in)
- wire rack

ICA Tip

Soya margarine works well in this recipe, and is soft enough to allow you to just put everything together in the mixer and mix until well combined.

1. Preheat oven to 180°C/350°F/Gas 4. Grease the bottom of a shallow tin and line with baking parchment.

2. Cream the butter or margarine together with the sugar until light and fluffy. Beat eggs and vanilla extract together and gradually beat into the creamed mixture.

3. Sieve the flour into a separate bowl before folding into the mixture along with the raisins and Kellogg's All-Bran or All-Bran Buds. Turn mixture into tin and spread so it is level. Bake in preheated oven for about 45 minutes. Turn out to cool on a wire rack.

4. To make the glacé icing, sieve the icing sugar into a bowl and stir in enough hot water to bind it to a fairly thick consistency. Spread over the cake and allow to set before cutting into 16 bars. Store in an airtight container, where they will keep well for at least a week.

Orange Chocolate Bars

MARGARET SIDES, LONGFORD

These family favourites were so popular for birthdays and special occasions that I used to have to put them out of reach, which didn't stop my son from climbing on a chair to get them when I wasn't looking.

Makes 2 trays of bars

- 225g (8oz) self-raising flour
- 4 level tablespoons cocoa powder
- 170g (6oz) porridge oatmeal
- 110g (4oz) sugar
- 225g (8oz) margarine

for the icing

- 225g (8oz) icing sugar
- 6 dessertspoons orange juice
- 4 teaspoons cocoa powder

what you'll need

- two 23cm x 32½cm (9in x 13in) Swiss roll tins
- wire rack

ICA Tip
These bars freeze well, making them handy for baking in larger batches.

1. Preheat oven to 180°C/350°F/Gas 4. Prepare two Swiss roll tins by greasing or lining with baking parchment.

2. Sieve the flour and cocoa into a large mixing bowl and stir in the oatmeal and sugar. Melt the margarine in a saucepan and pour over the dry ingredients, mixing well.

3. Pour into two prepared baking tins and smooth out with a palette knife. Bake in preheated oven for about 25 minutes before transferring to a wire rack to cool.

4. When the bar bases are cool, make up the icing one batch at a time. Mix together half the sugar, orange juice and cocoa powder and smooth over the first bar base, marking out lines on the icing for dividing into squares or rectangles of required size. Set aside to harden and repeat with the remaining icing ingredients for the second base.

5. Once the icing has hardened, cut into bars along the markings. Store in an airtight container, where they will keep well for about a week.

Washing-up Blessing

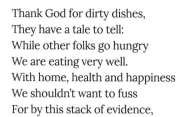

Thank God for dirty dishes,
They have a tale to tell:
While other folks go hungry
We are eating very well.
With home, health and happiness
We shouldn't want to fuss
For by this stack of evidence,
God's very good to us.

– Author unknown

"Work is the best way of passing the time."

– Anthony Cronin

"Work is love made visible."

– Kahlil Gibran

Maltesers Rocky Road

MAURA MOHAN, MONAGHAN

Who doesn't love a rocky road? The inclusion of Maltesers in this version makes for an extra treat – perfect for an energy boost on a busy day.

Makes 16
- 250g (9oz) chocolate
- 50g (2oz) butter
- 8 digestive biscuits
- 175g (6oz) Maltesers
- 60g (2oz) mini marshmallows

to finish
- icing sugar, for dusting

what you'll need
- 22cm square tin

1. Line a square tin with baking parchment.

2. Place a large heatproof bowl over a pot of boiling water and gently melt the chocolate and butter together. Remove from the heat and set aside to cool for about 10 minutes.

3. Meanwhile, bash up the biscuits in a plastic bag until you have a good mixture of chunks and powder. Add the crushed biscuits, Maltesers and marshmallows to the chocolate mixture, folding in with a spoon until everything is covered in chocolate.

4. Pour into prepared tin and refrigerate for at least 30 minutes. Sieve some icing sugar over the set mixture and slice into even chunks before serving.

"A person's actions will tell you everything you need to know."

– Anonymous

I love a house that's lived in
With clutter here and there –
A magazine left open,
A jacket on a chair.
A smell of something baking
(A special recipe)
An ever-eager offer of hospitality.

I love a house that's lived in.
It seems to stand apart:

For in it is a woman
Who has a loving heart.

– Author unknown

"Forget your perfect offering
There is a crack in everything
That's how the light gets in."

– Leonard Cohen

Begin at the beginning...

Chapter 2
Quiet Days

"Tea should be taken in solitude."
– C.S. Lewis

The ICA is built on principles of community and sharing, on practical skills and action. But we are no busy fools, and we understand the value of stepping out of the currents of daily life and pausing, of taking some time alone. Whether through conscious prayer or the contentment of craftwork, through the daily ritual of making the perfect pot of tea or meditative baking and bread-making practices, there are many ways to slow the pace down enough to really hear ourselves think.

"The unexamined life is not worth living."

– Socrates

That pause allows us time to reflect; it brings us back to the present moment, the here and now. And it is by making the time and space for ourselves, and noticing the world around us, that we feel gratitude for and find inspiration in all that we have. We need to recharge our energy in order to be better able to give of ourselves. And we need time to reflect in order to know how to act.

"The truth is rarely pure, and never simple."

– Oscar Wilde

Even in the quietest of times, however, we do not have to feel alone. Whether we want to enter another life through the pages of a favourite book or simply connect with another's heart and soul through remembering a few treasured lines, the gift of words allows us to engage with others even when alone.

"Tea is the magic key to the vault where my brain is kept."

– Frances Hardinge

Make Some Moments

Make some moments for yourself each day,
Some hour, some minutes you can call your own,
To free your mind of worries, of daily cares,
To set your heart at ease,
To be alone.
And you will find yourself
Refreshed,
Renewed,
Revitalised
In all you think and do.

– Author unknown

" Life will keep bringing you the same test
over and over again until you pass it. "

– Anonymous

" You can never get a cup of tea large
enough or a book long enough to suit me. "

– C.S. Lewis

Scones with Raspberry Jam

EDWARD HAYDEN, ICA COOKERY TUTOR

You can't beat fresh homemade scones – unless you serve them with homemade raspberry jam, which just hits the spot every time. If you don't already have a stand-by scone recipe up your sleeve, this one's for you.

Makes 12
- 450g (1lb) plain flour
- 1 level teaspoon baking powder
- pinch of salt
- 85g (3oz) caster sugar
- 85g (3oz) cold butter, cut into small pieces
- 1 egg
- 150ml (¼ pint) milk, approximately

to finish
- 1 egg, beaten
- a little extra milk
- granulated sugar, for sprinkling
- icing sugar, for dusting

to serve
- homemade raspberry jam (see p30 for recipe)
- freshly whipped cream
- a handful of strawberries, sliced thinly (optional)

what you'll need
- scone cutter
- baking tray
- wire rack

1. Preheat oven to 190°C/375°F/Gas 5. Line a baking tray with baking parchment.

2. Sieve the flour and baking powder together into a large mixing bowl. Add the salt and caster sugar to the mix, and rub in the butter with your fingertips.

3. Beat the egg in a separate bowl and add to the dry ingredients. Gradually add the milk, mixing together as you do so to form a soft dough. You may not need all of the milk. If the mixture becomes too wet and loose, add in a little extra flour.

4. Transfer to a floured surface and flatten out to about 2cm in depth. Using a scone cutter, cut out some shapes and transfer them to prepared baking tray.

5. Make up a little egg wash by beating an egg with some milk and brush this over the top of the scones. Sprinkle with a little granulated sugar and bake in preheated oven for 17–20 minutes or until golden brown.

6. Remove from the oven to a wire rack and dust with icing sugar. Serve warm or cold with homemade raspberry jam and freshly whipped cream. A strawberry can look quite pretty sliced on the top.

Raspberry Jam

EDWARD HAYDEN, ICA COOKERY TUTOR

I simply love the taste of homemade raspberry jam, but you could vary the fruit used. The lemon juice acts as the setting agent; it sets the jam with its natural pectin.

Makes 2 jars

- 450g (1lb) raspberries, fresh or frozen
- 450g (1lb) caster sugar
- ½ lemon, juice only
- 50ml (2fl oz) water

what you'll need

- 2 jam jars
- baking parchment
- string or rubber bands
- labels

ICA Tip

This same basic recipe can be applied to any type of fruit to make a delicious jam for any season – try it with gooseberries, blackcurrants or rhubarb and ginger root.

1. Combine all ingredients in a large pot and bring to the boil. Reduce the heat and simmer for about 20 minutes or until a spoon of jam sets on a chilled saucer. This will indicate that the jam is ready to be transferred to the jars.

2. Meanwhile, sterilise the jars. Preheat oven to 110°C/225°F/Gas ¼. Soak the jars in hot soapy water to remove labels and wash clean several times, rinsing thoroughly. Fill jars with boiling water and leave for two minutes before emptying. Transfer to preheated oven for 20 minutes to dry fully.

3. Once jam has reached setting point, transfer to sterilised jars and cover each immediately with a piece of baking parchment secured with string or rubber bands. Label with the name and date, and use as required. The jam will remain fresh for a good six months.

"My maternal grandmother was a great lover of poetry and threw lines of poems about whenever they could slot into the conversations of the day.... I think poetry is easier to recall than even great prose. Whether we leave 'footprints on the sands of time' or not, we would do well to remember lines from W.H. Davies's 'Leisure':

What is this life if, full of care,
we have no time to stand and stare.

I think if we could say the 'Serenity Prayer' – and really mean it and believe it – we'd all be on the way to complete happiness. "

– Anne Carleton, Cork

from Serenity Prayer

God, give me grace to accept with serenity
the things that cannot be changed,
courage to change the things
which should be changed,
and the wisdom to distinguish
the one from the other.

Living one day at a time,
Enjoying one moment at a time,
Accepting hardship as a pathway to peace.

– from an early version by Reinhold Niebuhr

"Nothing wastes more energy than worrying.
The longer one carries a problem, the heavier it gets.
Don't take things too seriously.
Live a life of serenity, not a life of regrets. "

– Douglas Pagels

Iris's Idiot-proof Brown Bread

IRIS FARRELL, LOUTH

I grew up in an era when everyone had a recipe for brown bread.
Some would share their secret – a handful of this and a handful of that
– but my bread would turn out nothing like the bread served at their table.
For years I tried every recipe I could find, and for years even the birds in the
garden refused to eat my bread. Eventually, I came upon a version that seemed
to break all the rules. And, would you believe, I finally baked the perfect
brown bread! I have passed this recipe on to literally hundreds of people
and I am so proud when people tell me they are still
baking and enjoying Iris's Bread.

Makes 900g (2lb) loaf

- 170g (6oz) fine wheaten flour
- 50g (2oz) plain flour
- 25g (1oz) bran
- 25g (1oz) wheat germ
- 25g (1oz) oatmeal
- 25g (1oz) pinhead oatmeal
- 2 teaspoons sugar (or sweetener of choice)
- 1 teaspoon bicarbonate of soda
- pinch of salt
- 1 egg
- 400ml (¾ pint) fresh milk or water
- 1 tablespoon olive oil (optional)

what you'll need

- 900g (2lb) loaf tin
- wire rack

1. Preheat oven to 180°C/350°F/Gas 4. Prepare the loaf tin by greasing lightly and dusting with flour or lining the base with baking parchment.

2. Combine all dry ingredients in a large mixing jug or bowl, stirring to mix well.

3. Beat egg in a separate jug or bowl together with the milk or water, and olive oil if using. Once combined, add to the dry ingredients, stirring to mix well.

4. Pour into prepared loaf tin and bake for one hour in preheated oven. Remove from tin to cool on a wire rack.

Wheat-free Brown Bread

AN GRIANÁN, LOUTH

This recipe is suitable for anyone with a wheat or dairy intolerance. It's a nice one to bake on a quiet day and freeze for use when needed.

Makes 450g (1lb) loaf
- 450g (1lb) medium oatmeal
- 50g (2oz) pinhead oatmeal
- 3 tablespoons sunflower seeds
- 1 teaspoon bicarbonate of soda
- ½ teaspoon salt
- 400ml (¾ pint) soya milk, approximately
- 2 tablespoons oil

what you'll need
- 450g (1lb) loaf tin
- wire rack

ICA Tip
You can also use yofu (soy-based yoghurt) in lieu of the soya milk for this recipe.

1. Preheat oven to 200°C/400°F/Gas 6. Lightly grease the loaf tin.

2. Combine all dry ingredients in a large mixing bowl, add the liquids and mix together well. You're aiming for a loose mixture, so add more or less soya milk as needed. Pour into prepared loaf tin.

3. Bake in preheated oven for 60 minutes, reducing the heat to 180°C/350°F/Gas 4 after 20 minutes if it looks like the top is browning too quickly. Remove from tin to cool on a wire rack.

Night

In the night silence,
God is whispering to us,
In the rustling leaves.

The light of the moon
Reflects the divine presence
And blesses us all.

The cows in the barn
Chew contentedly.
The world is at peace.

– Peg Prendeville, Limerick

"We need silence to be able to touch souls."

– Mother Teresa

"Breathing is wealth, and being alive is hope."

– Anonymous

Guinness Bread

MAURA RIORDAN, DUBLIN

Although a great recipe for St Patrick's Day, I love this all year round.
It is particularly good with smoked Irish salmon, surely one of the
great delicacies of the world.

Makes 900g (2lb) loaf
- 450g (1lb) coarse wholemeal flour
- 25g (1oz) pinhead oatmeal
- 4 tablespoons demerara sugar
- 2 level teaspoons bicarbonate of soda
- 50g (2oz) butter
- 1 tablespoon treacle
- 400ml (¾ pint) Guinness

what you'll need
- 900g (2lb) loaf tin

1. Preheat oven to 190°C/375°F/Gas 5. Lightly grease the loaf tin.

2. Combine the dry ingredients in a large mixing bowl, sieving in the bicarbonate of soda.

3. Melt the butter and treacle in a saucepan over low heat. Remove from the heat, add the Guinness and mix well.

4. Pour into mixing bowl with dry ingredients and mix well until combined. Bake in preheated oven for 45–50 minutes. Remove from tin and wrap in a clean tea towel, and allow to cool before cutting. (Cooling in the tea towel improves the crust.)

from Bread

Someone else cut off my head
In a golden field.
Now I am re-created

By her fingers. This
Moulding is more delicate
Than a first kiss,

More deliberate than her own
Rising up
And lying down.

Even at my weakest, I am
Finer than anything
In this legendary garden.

Yet I am nothing till
She runs her fingers through me
And shapes me with her skill.
...

So I am glad to go through fire
And come out

Shaped like her dream.
In my way
I am all that can happen to men.
I came to life at her fingerends.
I will go back into her again.

– Brendan Kennelly

Milk Rolls

BELTRA GUILD MEMBERS, SLIGO

A simple dinner accompaniment for simple days.

- 225g (8oz) self-raising flour
- 1 teaspoon baking powder
- pinch of salt
- 50g (2oz) butter, cut into small squares
- 1 tablespoon caster sugar
- 1 egg, beaten
- 125ml (4fl oz) fresh milk, approximately

to finish
- 1 egg, beaten

what you'll need
- baking tray or sheet
- wire rack

1. Preheat oven to 200°C/400°F/Gas 6. Grease a baking tray or sheet.

2. Sieve the flour and baking powder into a large mixing bowl. Add the salt and butter and rub in well.

3. Add the sugar, beaten egg and just enough milk to make an elastic dough.

4. Roll out to 1cm (1½in) thick, cut into triangles and roll up each of these from its base towards its point.

5. Transfer to prepared baking tray, brush with a little beaten egg and bake in preheated oven for 15–20 minutes. Transfer to a wire rack to cool.

"My first-ever drop scone was made for me by my mother's good friend, who was working as a housekeeper in Blackrock in Dublin. I remember vividly her methodical process of making the mix. I would sit beside my mother and watch in awe as she created these delicious treats in what seemed to be the grandest frying pan ever seen.

She made an abundance of scones in batches of three. Each finished set was placed into a tea towel that sat on a warmed plate at the side of the Aga cooker.

All the while, my mother and her friend chatted and reminisced, and I listened and wished for a taste of these scones, which were in my mind no longer just scones but a little piece of homely warmth and goodness. And, oh my, were they delicious with melting butter and homemade strawberry jam!

My two children and I now enjoy making these together – the chatting, the laughter, the cooking, the dreaming – and when they are ready we sit down together at the table, tuck in and talk some more. "

– Margaret Bowkett, Wexford

"May you live all the days of your life."

– Jonathan Swift

Drop Scones

MARGARET BOWKETT, WEXFORD

I learned to make these drop scones from my mother's housekeeper friend. We used to eat them with melting butter and homemade jam, but they are also delicious with honey, lemon juice and sugar or chocolate sauce. The choices are endless!

Makes about 10–12

- 250g (9oz) plain flour
- ½ teaspoon bicarbonate of soda
- ½ teaspoon cream of tartar
- 1 large egg, beaten
- 275ml (½ pint) buttermilk
- vegetable oil, for greasing the pan

to serve

- lashings of butter
- your choice of topping

what you'll need

- heavy-based frying pan

1. Sieve the dry ingredients into a large mixing bowl. Stir in the beaten egg followed by the buttermilk and mix until everything is well integrated.

2. Grease a heavy-based frying pan with vegetable oil and heat it well. Reduce the heat slightly and drop spoonfuls of the mixture onto the hot pan, taking care not to overcrowd it – batches of three work well, depending on the size of your pan.

3. When bubbles appear on the top of your scones, flip them over to cook the other side. Once golden brown on both sides, transfer them from the pan onto a clean tea towel. Wrap them in the towel and set aside somewhere warm to keep them warm and steamy.

4. Serve with butter and your choice of delicious topping.

from The Lake Isle of Innisfree

I will arise and go now, and go to Innisfree,
And a small cabin build there, of clay and wattles made:
Nine bean-rows will I have there, a hive for the honey bee,
And live alone in the bee-loud glade.

And I shall have some peace there, for peace comes dropping slow,
Dropping from the veils of the morning to where the cricket sings;
There midnight's all a glimmer, and noon a purple glow,
And evening full of the linnet's wings.

W.B. Yeats

" Forget past, future, good and bad;
Stay only in the present. "

– Anonymous

44

Battenberg Cake

BELTRA GUILD MEMBERS, SLIGO

Sometimes called church window cake – for obvious reasons – this is best baked when you have some time on your hands and you can pop on some peaceful music and enjoy the process.

Makes 20cm x 10cm
(8in x 4in) cake

- 170g (6oz) margarine
- 140g (5oz) caster sugar
- 3 eggs, beaten rigorously
- 170g (6oz) self-raising flour
- 2–3 drops red food colouring
- 5–6 tablespoons apricot jam
- 600g marzipan, ready-made or see p146 for recipe

what you'll need

- 20cm (8in) square baking tin
- wire rack
- pastry brush

ICA Tip

If you leave the baked sponge overnight before cutting, it will be much easier to cut.

1. Preheat oven to 170°C/325°F/Gas 3. One of the biggest challenges is to line the tin properly. Grease and line the square tin with baking parchment. Divide the tin in half with a strip of foil folded into a double thickness. This will allow you to bake the two halves separately.

2. In a large mixing bowl, beat the margarine and sugar to a soft cream. Gradually add the beaten eggs and flour to the mixture, adding in a little of each alternately. Beat to a smooth batter.

3. Transfer half of the batter into a second bowl, and colour this pink with a few drops of red food colouring. Pour the separate batches of batter into each side of the baking tin and bake in preheated oven for 40-50 minutes, or until a skewer inserted into the cake comes out clean. Turn onto a wire rack and leave until quite cold. Cut each sponge lengthways into two perfectly rectangular strips, trimming if necessary to ensure equal sides.

4. Taking one pink and one white strip, brush one length of each with jam loosened with a little hot water. Press together to form the base. Brush over with jam, top with two more strips (the plain strip on top of the pink and vice versa) and press together to bind. Place a dish, or a tin with a small weight in it, on top of the cake and leave for an hour.

5. Meanwhile, make the marzipan if not using shop-bought paste. Measure the outer surface of the cake. Roll the almond paste out on a sugared surface, aiming for a piece large enough to cover the cake completely.

6. Brush the top and sides of the cake with jam and place top-down on the paste. Brush the final side of the cake with jam and wrap the paste around, pressing to secure. Pinch to seal the join and then pinch the edges to define the shape. Cut into slices to serve.

Watch your thoughts; they become your words.
Watch your words; they become your actions.
Watch your actions; they become your habits.
Watch your habits; they become your character.
Watch your character; it becomes your destiny.

– Author unknown

" Care about what other people think
and you will always be their prisoner. "

– Lao-Tzu

" When you cease to fear your solitude, a new creativity
awakens in you. Your forgotten or neglected wealth
begins to reveal itself. "

– John O'Donohue

May you live
all the days
of your life

Chapter 3
Difficult Days

"Friendship... is not something you learn in school. But if you haven't learned
the meaning of friendship, you really haven't learned anything."
– Muhammad Ali

Sometimes it takes the most difficult of life's challenges to remind us of the value of community and friendship. But once we have learned firsthand the power of such simple words as "Can I help?" or "I'm sorry for your troubles" spoken with sincerity, it is a lesson we rarely forget. It is often said that we Irish are at our best under adversity, and certainly we have a strong tradition of coming together as communities when individuals amongst us need help processing the pain of loss and grief.

> " Blessed are they that mourn:
> for they shall be comforted. "
>
> – Matthew 5:4

There are many ways to show someone that you are there for them. Often we turn to the most pressing practicalities, such as feeding and watering the people who have come together to mourn someone's passing. The making and serving of endless pots of tea, trays of sandwiches and slices of fruit cake or apple pie are really acts of love. And when the crowds have gone, a gift-wrapped package of homemade biscuits can be a great excuse for a quick visit to remind someone you haven't forgotten their sorrow.

> " Tough times never last,
> but tough people do. "
>
> – Robert Schuller

Being a friend to someone means that we can offer them a fresh perspective. Being less consumed by the pain that they are facing, we can remind them that all things will eventually pass and that we will still be standing beside them. We cannot take their pain away, but we can make it that little bit easier for them to bear, just by being a witness to it. It is good to remember, and perhaps to mention to those in pain, that sometimes the most painful times are those of transformative change, and that the growth involved in change can bring much that is good.

> " In a crisis, be aware of the dangers,
> but recognise the opportunities. "
>
> – John F. Kennedy

"During the Celtic Tiger years a lot of money poured into my neighbourhood as land was sold for enormous amounts to build housing estates, shops and apartments. Our children began to see this money in their friends' pockets and households. One of our children got a little plaque with the saying 'The best thing to spend on your children is love.' The word love had been crossed out with black marker and the saying now read, 'The best thing to spend on your children is money.'

Our children began to ask us if we were rich. In response, I coined a phrase in our home that although we were not rich in terms of money, we were 'rich in love'. This became our stock answer when peer pressure was huge and friends were able to buy anything they wanted.

During really difficult times, when our children learned that they could not get everything they asked for, I regularly made their favourite chocolate cake. It was made with love and, as we sat down to eat, I hoped that they felt this love and that they would treasure these times in later life."

– Caroline Power, Meath

"Life is a test, give it your best,
stand up with your back to the wall.
Laugh and don't cry, never say die,
get up again when you fall."

– Author unknown

"Pick yourself up,
Dust yourself off,
Start all over again."

– Dorothy Fields

Rich-in-Love Chocolate Cake

CAROLINE POWER, MEATH

Made and served with love, this cake always helped our family get through difficult days. I hope it works its magic for you and your loved ones.

Makes 20cm (8in) cake
- 4 eggs
- 50g (2oz) plain flour
- 50g (2oz) cornflour
- 25g (1oz) cocoa powder
- 1 level teaspoon baking powder
- pinch of salt
- 110g (4oz) caster sugar

to finish
- 1–2 chocolate flake bars
- 275ml (½ pint) cream

what you'll need
- 2 x 20cm (8in) Swiss roll tins
- wire rack

1. Preheat oven to 200°C/400°F/Gas 6. Grease two Swiss roll tins.

2. Separate the eggs and set aside the yolks and whites. Sieve the flour, cornflour, cocoa, baking powder and salt together in a mixing bowl.

3. Beat egg whites in a large bowl until stiff and peaky. Gradually add the sugar, whisking until smooth, and then whisk in the egg yolks.

4. Quickly and lightly fold in sieved ingredients with a metal spoon and divide mixture evenly between prepared sandwich tins. Bake in preheated oven for 15 minutes before transferring to a wire rack to cool.

5. Break up the flake bars into small pieces. Whip the cream until it forms soft peaks and add the chocolate. When the cake is fully cool, spread the cream mixture on one layer and place the other layer on top.

When things go wrong, as they sometimes will,
When the road you're trudging seems all uphill,
When the funds are low and the debts are high,
And you want to smile, but you have to sigh,
When care is pressing you down a bit,
Rest if you must, but don't you quit.

– Author unknown

**"Walking with a friend in the dark
is better than walking alone in the light."**

– Helen Keller

**"How sad would be November if you
had no knowledge of the spring."**

– Edwin Way Teale

THANK YOU

Chocolate Swiss Roll

BELTRA GUILD MEMBERS, SLIGO

Sometimes there's real comfort to be found in old-fashioned treats, and there's nothing like a chocolate Swiss roll for indulging in nostalgia.

Serves 6–8

- 2 eggs
- 85g (3oz) caster sugar
- 50g (2oz) plain chocolate
- 50g (2oz) plain flour
- 1 teaspoon vanilla extract

for the filling

- 7g (¼oz) gelatine
- 2 teaspoons milk, warmed
- 1 egg white
- 1 dessertspoon caster sugar
- 2 tablespoons cream
- 12 drops vanilla extract

to dust the sponge

- icing sugar

what you'll need

- 23cm x 32½cm (9in x 13in) Swiss roll tin

ICA Tip

If you're planning to serve the Swiss roll immediately or to pregnant women or people with compromised immune systems, you can simply fill with freshly whipped cream sweetened with a little sugar and vanilla, but the egg white and gelatine allow the cake to hold its shape better.

1. Preheat oven to 200°C/400°F/Gas 6. Prepare a Swiss roll tin by greasing with butter and dusting with sugar and flour.

2. Place a large heatproof bowl over a pot of boiling water. Add the eggs and sugar and whisk gently for about 15–20 minutes or until the mixture emulsifies. Remove bowl from over the boiling water.

3. In a separate heatproof bowl, melt chocolate over the pot of boiling water. Add the chocolate to the egg and sugar mixture, stirring well to mix.

4. Sieve in the flour and add the vanilla, stirring until quite smooth. Pour the mixture into prepared baking tin and bake in preheated oven for 10–15 minutes.

5. Remove from oven and turn out onto baking parchment dusted with sieved icing sugar. Roll up loosely and set aside to cool.

6. Meanwhile, prepare the filling. Dissolve the gelatine in the warmed milk and set aside to cool. Whisk the egg white together with the caster sugar until quite stiff. In a separate bowl, whisk the cream until thick. When the gelatine is fully cool, mix into whisked cream, add the vanilla and fold in the beaten egg white and sugar. Mix well.

7. When the sponge is almost cold, unroll very carefully. Spread with the filling and gently re-roll. Dust with a little extra icing sugar and serve.

Coffee Ring Cake

LIZ WALL, WICKLOW

Be sure to use the best coffee you can for this simple but delicious cake. Careful sourcing really does make a difference.

Makes 20cm (8in) ring cake
- 3 large eggs
- 110g (4oz) caster sugar
- 1 tablespoon very strong, hot coffee
- 85g (3oz) self-raising flour, sieved

for the icing
- 225g (8oz) icing sugar, sieved
- 1½ tablespoons very strong, hot coffee

what you'll need
- ring tin, 20cm (8in) wide and 7½cm (3in) deep

1. Preheat oven to 180°C/350°F/Gas 4. Grease the ring tin.

2. With an electric whisk, whisk the eggs and sugar together very hard for at least five minutes, until thick.

3. Add the coffee and gently fold in the sieved flour. Pour into the prepared ring tin and bake in the centre of the preheated oven for 30–35 minutes until well risen, firm to the touch and just shrinking from the sides of the tin. Cool before turning out.

4. Meanwhile, to make the coffee icing, combine the icing sugar and coffee in a small pan. Heat very gently, all the while mixing with a wooden spoon until smooth. Pour over the coffee ring cake and allow to set.

> " Too often, we underestimate the power of a touch,
> a smile, a kind word, a listening ear. "

– Author unknown

> " After the death of my husband Sean, a friend and
> fellow ICA member Kathleen emailed me the poem 'God's Phone Number'.
> It was a kind and lovely thought and was much appreciated. "

– Sally Dunleavy, Mayo

God's Phone Number

Hello, God, I called tonight to talk a little while.
I need a friend who'll listen to my anxiety and trial.
You see, I can't quite make it through a day just on my own.
I need your love to guide me so I'll never feel alone.

I want to ask you please to keep my family safe and sound.
Come and fill their lives with confidence for whatever fate
they're bound.
Give me faith, dear God, to face each hour through the day,
And not to worry over things I can't change in any way.

I thank you, God, for being home and listening to my call,
For giving me such good advice when I stumble and fall.
Your number is the only one that answers every time;
I never get a busy signal and never have to pay a dime.

So thank you, God, for listening to my troubles and my sorrow.
Good night, God, I love you too and I'll call again tomorrow.

– Author unknown

Flour-free Fruit Cake

NORA RYAN, SLIGO

This flour-free cake uses ground almonds in place of the usual flour base, making it suitable for coeliacs and gluten-free diets. More importantly, it tastes delicious and is light and lovely enough to convert fruit cake sceptics.

Makes 20cm (8in) cake

- 170g (6oz) raisins
- 85g (3oz) chopped dates
- 2 dessertspoons sweet sherry
- 340g (12oz) ground almonds
- 170g (6oz) glacé cherries, quartered
- 170g (6oz) butter
- 170g (6oz) caster sugar
- 6 eggs
- 1 teaspoon almond essence

what you'll need

- 20cm (8in) round cake tin
- wire rack

1. Preheat oven to 170°C/325°F/Gas 3. Lightly grease the round cake tin.

2. Combine the raisins, dates and sherry in a saucepan and heat gently over a low heat until the fruit soaks up the alcohol. Transfer to a bowl to cool before adding three tablespoons of ground almonds along with the glacé cherries and tossing together.

3. In a separate bowl, cream the butter and sugar until soft and fluffy. Separate the eggs and set aside the whites. Beat the egg yolks into the butter and sugar mix, together with the almond essence. Stir in the remaining ground almonds and the soaked fruit and set aside.

4. In a separate bowl, whisk egg whites until stiff but not dry. With a metal spoon, fold one third of the beaten egg whites into the cake mixture and mix thoroughly before gently folding in the remaining egg whites.

5. Pour the mixture into a prepared tin and bake in preheated oven for 50–60 minutes or until a skewer inserted into cake comes out clean. Transfer to a wire rack to cool.

Apple & Rhubarb Pie

AN GRIANÁN, LOUTH

If there's comfort in the familiar, then how comforting is the sight and smell of an apple pie, whether fresh from the oven or delivered wrapped in foil for reheating. This version has the added element of rhubarb for a seasonal treat.

Makes one 20cm (8in) pie
- 225g (8oz) plain flour
- 1 teaspoon caster sugar
- 140g (5oz) margarine or butter
- 1 egg, beaten
- a little milk, for brushing

for the filling
- 450g (1lb) ripe rhubarb
- 3 cooking apples
- 350g (12oz) caster sugar

what you'll need
- 20cm (8in) ovenproof pie dish or plate

1. Sieve the flour into a large mixing bowl, add the sugar and margarine, and rub together to resemble breadcrumbs. Mix in the beaten egg to bind pastry together, adding a tablespoon or two of cold water if the mixture is still too dry. It should be firm but rollable. Wrap in cling film and chill for several hours (or overnight) in the fridge.

2. Preheat oven to 180°C/350°F/Gas 4 and lightly grease the ovenproof pie dish. Divide pastry in two, allowing slightly more for the base. Roll the larger piece out on a lightly floured surface and transfer to the base of the pie dish. Trim the edges of the pastry with a sharp knife and dampen the rim with a pastry brush dipped in cold water. Roll out the rest of the pastry.

3. Chop the rhubarb into small slices about 1cm (½in) thick. Peel, core and chop the apples into similar sized slices. Fill the pie with fruit, sprinkle generously with the sugar to taste and top with the second round of pastry. Press the edges down with your thumb to seal and use a fork to crimp around the sides. Trim with a sharp knife and prick the top of the pie a couple of times.

4. Brush top with milk for a golden colour. Bake in preheated oven for 50–60 minutes or until the pastry is golden and the rhubarb has softened and is cooked through.

"Count your blessings, not your troubles.
You'll make it through whatever comes along.
Within you are so many answers.
Understand, have courage, be strong."

– Douglas Pagels

"Gratitude is something of which none of us can give too
much: for on the smiles, the thanks we give, our little
gestures of appreciation, our neighbours build their
philosophy of life."

– A.J. Cronin

"Courage is the price that
Life exacts for granting peace.
The soul that knows it not
Knows no release from little things."

– Amelia Earhart

Marmalade Shortcakes

BELTRA GUILD MEMBERS, SLIGO

These sweet-and-sour shortcakes would make a thoughtful gift for a friend to show you care. They store well in an airtight container, so consider doubling the batch and keeping some for yourself too.

Makes about 10–12 biscuits
- 225g (8oz) flour
- 85g (3oz) caster sugar
- pinch of salt
- 110g (4oz) butter or margarine, cut into pieces
- 1 tablespoon milk

for the filling
- your favourite marmalade (or jam)

what you'll need
- baking tray or sheet
- biscuit cutter
- sweet cutter or sturdy straw
- wire rack

1. Preheat oven to 180°C/350°F/Gas 4. Lightly grease a baking tray or sheet, or line with baking parchment.

2. In a large mixing bowl, combine the flour, sugar and salt, and mix well. Add the butter or margarine, and rub into the flour with fingertips until it is evenly distributed.

3. Add just enough milk to bind (you may need less than a tablespoon or a little more) and knead into a smooth dough. Roll out on a lightly floured surface and, using the biscuit cutter, cut into round biscuits. Transfer half of the biscuits to prepared baking tray or sheet and spread a layer of marmalade on each.

4. In the centre of each of the remaining biscuits, cut three small round holes with a sweet cutter or sturdy straw. Place the perforated biscuits on top of the jam-coated biscuits and bake in preheated oven for 20–30 minutes, or until golden brown.

5. Transfer to a wire rack to cool and store in an airtight container.

Chocolate Florentines

NELLIE DILLON, KILDARE

There are many ways to show someone you care and remind them that you are thinking of them, but few are as delicious as these Chocolate Florentines. This recipe was picked up in Spain, where almonds are sweet and plentiful.

Makes about 40
- 250g (9oz) flaked almonds
- 200g (7oz) sugar
- 150g (5oz) glucose (sold in powdered form in chemists)
- 100g (3½oz) butter
- 50ml (2fl oz) cream
- 1 orange, grated rind only

to finish
- 300g chocolate, dark or milk

what you'll need
- baking tray or silicone sheet
- wire rack

ICA Tip
The caramel base means these will keep well for up to a week if stored in an airtight container.

1. Preheat oven to 180°C/350°F/Gas 4. If using a baking tray, line it with baking parchment.

2. Combine the almonds, sugar, glucose, butter, cream and grated orange rind in a non-stick pot. Heat over a medium heat, stirring with a wooden spoon until well integrated.

3. Remove the caramel from the heat and leave to cool until it is thick but malleable. Shape the mixture into balls the size of large hazelnuts and place onto lined baking tray or silicone sheet, keeping them about 3cm apart as they will spread. Bake in preheated oven for 15–20 minutes or until the edges are golden. Remove from the oven and set aside until cooled.

4. Meanwhile, place a large heatproof bowl over a pot of boiling water and gently melt the chocolate.

5. Once the bases are cool, place them on a wire rack where you can coat each individually with the melted chocolate. Allow to set before storing in an airtight container.

A Friendship Blessing

May you be blessed with good friends.
May you learn to be a good friend to yourself.
May you be able to journey to that place in your soul where there is great
    love, warmth, feeling and forgiveness.
May this change you.
May it transfigure that which is negative, distant or cold in you.
May you be brought in to the real passion, kinship and affinity of belonging.
May you treasure your friends.
May you be good to them and may you be there for them; may they bring
    you all the blessings, challenges, truth and light that you need for
    your journey.
May you never be isolated.
May you always be in the gentle nest of belonging with your *anam cara*.

– John O'Donohue

" Many people will walk in and out of your life, but only
true friends will leave footprints in your heart. "

– Eleanor Roosevelt

" Think where man's glory most begins and ends,
and say my glory was I had such friends. "

– W.B. Yeats

'Pick yourself
up,
Dust yourself off,
Start all over
again,'

Chapter 4
Precious Days

❦

"May your heart be warm and happy with the lilt of Irish laughter,
Every day in every way and forever and ever after."
– Irish blessing

So many Irish blessings wish not for wealth and comfort and material trappings but rather for those things that money cannot buy: happiness, joy, laughter, love. We achieve these things by investing our energy in what is most precious to us, by sharing time with our nearest and dearest. Precious memories – which sustain us when times are hard or when a loved one is no longer with us – must be made to begin with. We create them by celebrating life as we live it, by celebrating birthdays, marking milestones and remembering anniversaries.

> " You can shed tears that she is gone
> or you can smile because she has lived. "
>
> – Anonymous

No wonder that we have favourite family recipes for cakes and treats that are eaten on only the most special of occasions. Our senses of taste and smell are so closely linked to one another, and our sense of smell so closely linked to our memories that the ritual of making and sharing these recipes is a way for us to both encapsulate and release these memories. But of course sometimes the most precious memories of all are not of those special celebrations, but of the quieter times shared, of the ordinary moments that become extraordinary when infused with the generous light of love.

> " May you live as long as you want,
> And never want as long as you live. "
>
> – Irish blessing

May love and laughter light your days
And warm your heart and home.
May good and faithful friends be yours
Wherever you may roam.
May peace and plenty bless your world
With joy that long endures.
May all life's passing seasons
Bring the best to you and yours.

– Irish blessing

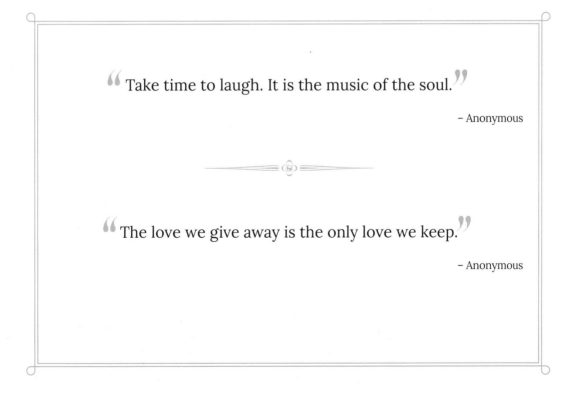

" Take time to laugh. It is the music of the soul. "

– Anonymous

" The love we give away is the only love we keep. "

– Anonymous

Mother's Malt Cake Loaf

ROSEMARY McCARVILLE, MONAGHAN

When I was a little girl, on cold winter evenings no treat was greater than to sit beside a roaring fire with a steaming mug of tea and Mammy's malt cake smothered in homemade butter churned from our own milk.

Makes two 450g (1lb) loaves

- 375g (13oz) sultanas
- 375ml (12fl oz) water, boiled
- 50g (2oz) butter or margarine
- 375g (13oz) self-raising flour
- ½ teaspoon bicarbonate of soda
- 250g (9oz) sugar
- 2 eggs, beaten

to serve

- farmhouse butter

what you'll need

- 2 x 450g (1lb) loaf tins
- wire rack

1. Preheat oven to 190°C/375°F/Gas 5. Grease two loaf tins.

2. Combine sultanas and butter in a saucepan with the boiled water. Return it to the boil and simmer for four minutes. Remove from the heat and allow to cool a little.

3. Mix together the flour, bicarbonate of soda and sugar, and mix in the beaten eggs. Stir in the cooled fruit and divide the mixture between the two prepared tins, levelling the top.

4. Bake in preheated oven for 60 minutes and then cool on a wire rack. Serve with lashings of farmhouse butter.

Nora De Buitléar's Special Occasion Dream Cake

MAMO McDONALD, MONAGHAN

I first tasted this cake in the 1970s at the ICA Diplomatic Luncheon for the female ambassadors to Ireland and the wives of male ambassadors. Nora agreed to share the recipe with me for my upcoming silver wedding "on account of the occasion". I copied it exactly into my notebook on 16 July 1975.

Serves 6–8

- 225g (8oz) dark chocolate
- 225g (8oz) butter or margarine
- 225g (8oz) plain biscuits, broken into pieces
- 50g (2oz) raisins (optional)
- 2 eggs, beaten
- 2 dessertspoons caster sugar
- rum, brandy or whiskey, to taste

to decorate

- walnuts or glacé cherries and angelica

what you'll need

- 20cm (8in) cake tin

1. Place a large heatproof bowl over a pot of boiling water and gently melt the chocolate. Melt the butter or margarine in a separate bowl.

2. Combine and add the broken biscuits, raisins, beaten eggs and sugar. Mix well and add the alcohol a little at a time, tasting the mixture until it's right (you'll probably be under the table by then).

3. Line the cake tin with baking parchment or clingfilm and fill with the cake mixture. Decorate with cherries and angelica or walnuts and leave in fridge overnight to set.

Cathryn's Crazy Chocolate Bake

MAMO McDONALD, MONAGHAN

This second chocolate biscuit cake is very family friendly. Our family loves the big get-togethers such as anniversaries, engagements and christenings. Everybody brings along a signature dish, ensuring plenty of variety. Just by watching the children you can see that Cathryn's Crazy Chocolate Bake is a clear winner every time.

Serves 6–8

- 350g (12oz) broken biscuits
- 285g (10oz) dark chocolate
- 110g (4oz) butter
- 1 can condensed milk
- 85g (3oz) nuts (optional)

what you'll need

- 23cm (9in) cake tin

ICA Tip

You can swap the nuts for raisins if you prefer.

1. Grease and line a cake tin with foil or cling film, leaving enough surplus to fold over the top. Break the biscuits into pieces and set aside.

2. Place a large heatproof bowl over a pot of boiling water and gently melt the chocolate together with the butter and milk. Mix in the broken biscuits and nuts and pour into the prepared cake tin. Fold the excess foil or cling film over the top of the mixture, press to flatten out and refrigerate overnight.

3. Remove from tin and unwrap. Slice into chunks and watch it disappear.

" Though we live in a world that dreams of ending
that always seems about to give in
something that will not acknowledge conclusion
insists that we forever begin. "

– Brendan Kennelly

" I thought I had forgotten how to hold a baby,
but my arms remember. "

– Anonymous

" Spread the feast, and let there be
Such music heard as best beseems
A king's son coming from the sea
To wed a maiden of the streams. "

– Francis Ledwidge

" Mothers hold their children's hands a while,
but their hearts forever. "

– Anonymous

Summer Fruit Family Slice

LIZ WALL, WICKLOW

It's arguable that life is too short to make your own puff pastry, especially when there's family time to enjoy. This quick and easy recipe will help you to make the most of that time together.

Serves 6

- 225g (8oz) shop-bought puff pastry
- 1 egg, beaten
- 450g (1lb) mixed soft summer fruits
- 2 heaped tablespoons caster sugar
- 150ml (¼ pint) double cream
- 1 vanilla pod, seeds only (optional)
- 1 heaped teaspoon icing sugar

for dusting

- plain flour
- icing sugar

what you'll need

- large baking tray
- wire rack

ICA Tip

If your pastry is too pale before glazing with sugar, brush again with egg and bake for an extra minute or two.

1. Preheat oven to 220°C/425°F/Gas 7. Prepare a large baking tray by lightly greasing or lining with baking parchment.

2. Roll out the pastry on a lightly floured surface into a 30cm x 24cm (12in x 9½in) rectangle. Transfer the pastry to the prepared baking tray, using the rolling pin to gently lift it up. Refrigerate for 20–30 minutes.

3. Once rested, prick the pastry with a fork and brush with beaten egg. Bake in preheated oven for 20–25 minutes or until lightly risen and golden brown.

4. Meanwhile, preheat the grill to hot. Cut the baked pastry lengthways into two rectangular strips. Dust each liberally with icing sugar and flash under preheated grill to lightly caramelise the sugar, taking care not to burn the pastry or your fingers. Repeat on the other side of each strip before transferring the crispy pastry strips to a wire rack to cool.

5. In a small saucepan, heat a couple of handfuls of the fruit with the caster sugar and a little water. Simmer gently for a few minutes before mashing lightly and straining through a sieve, using the back of a spoon to release all the juices from the pulp. Discard the pulp, return the juices to the heat and reduce to a syrupy consistency. Set aside.

6. Whip the double cream with the vanilla seeds, if using, and a heaped teaspoon of icing sugar until soft peaks form.

7. Place a pastry strip in the centre of a serving dish – this will be the base of your fruit sandwich. Pipe or spoon over half of the cream and top with fresh fruit, taking care not to overcrowd the filling. Drizzle over a little syrup, top with more cream and then the remaining strip of pastry. You can decorate the plate with any leftover fruit or serve this separately.

Crunchy Chocolate Meringue Cake

LIZ WALL, WICKLOW

This winning treat is all about contrasting textures: soft chewy meringue, crispy exterior, airy clouds of whipped cream and the crunch of finely chopped hazelnuts.

Serves 6–8
- 6 egg whites
- 350g (12oz) caster sugar
- 110g (4oz) hazelnuts, finely chopped

for the chocolate sauce
- 285g (10oz) dark or milk chocolate
- 375ml (12fl oz) double cream

what you'll need
- three 23cm x 32½cm (9in x 13in) Swiss roll tins

1. Preheat oven to 180°C/350°F/Gas 4. Line three Swiss roll tins with baking parchment.

2. In a large mixing bowl, whisk egg whites until stiff and then gradually whisk in sugar until mixture is glossy. Fold in chopped hazelnuts, reserving a few for decoration. Divide the mixture between the three prepared tins and bake in preheated oven for 30–35 minutes or until the meringue is crisp on the top. To ensure the layers cook at the same rate, move tins around the oven during baking.

3. Meanwhile, make the chocolate sauce. Break chocolate into a heavy-based pan, reserving a couple of squares for decoration. Add half of the cream and heat gently until chocolate has melted completely. Set aside to cool. Whip remaining cream and set aside.

4. Remove meringues from oven and leave in tins for one minute before carefully turning out and peeling away the parchment. The meringues should be crispy on top and soft underneath.

5. Place one meringue on a large serving plate, spread half of the chocolate sauce over it and smother the sauce with half of the whipped cream. Cover with the second meringue and repeat. Place last meringue on top and decorate with remaining nuts and some grated chocolate from the remaining squares.

Beatitudes for Friends of the Aged

Blessed are they who understand my faltering step and palsied hand.
Blessed are they who know that my ears today must strain to catch the things
    they say.
Blessed are they who seem to know that my eyes are dim and my wits are slow.
Blessed are they who looked away when coffee spilled on my table today.
Blessed are they with a cheery smile who stop to chat for a little while.
Blessed are they who never say, "You've told that story twice today."
Blessed are they who know the way to bring back memories of yesterday.
Blessed are they who make it known that I'm loved, respected and not alone.
Blessed are they who ease the days of my journey home in loving ways.

– Esther Mary Walker

" I love people who make me laugh.
I honestly think it's the thing I like to do most, to
laugh. It cures a multitude of ills. It's probably the most
important thing in a person. "

– Audrey Hepburn

" Maturity is a high price to pay for growing up. "

– Tom Stoppard

Gâteau Flamand

MARY M. SPILLANE, KERRY

This is my version of a 1960s Cordon Bleu recipe. It's quite time consuming so is really for visitors, but as it needs to be made at least a day in advance there is no last-minute pressure.

Makes 20cm (8in) flan
- 110g (4oz) flour
- pinch of salt
- 50g (2oz) butter
- 50g (2oz) caster sugar
- 2–3 drops vanilla extract
- 2 egg yolks
- 50g (2oz) crystallised cherries
- 3 tablespoons kirsch

for the frangipane filling
- 110g (4oz) butter
- 110g (4oz) caster sugar
- 2 eggs, lightly beaten
- 110g (4oz) ground almonds
- 25g (1oz) plain flour, sieved
- 1 tablespoon kirsch

to decorate
- 50g (2oz) flaked almonds
- 250g icing sugar
- 2–3 tablespoons just-boiled water

what you'll need
- 20cm (8in) diameter flan tin

1. To make the French flan pastry, sieve flour with salt onto a pastry board or into a large mixing bowl. Make a well in the centre and put in the butter, sugar, vanilla extract and egg yolks. Using the fingertips of one hand only, pinch and work the last four ingredients together until well blended and then draw in the flour to combine. Knead lightly until smooth.

2. Wrap in cling film and refrigerate for an hour or two. Meanwhile, slice the crystallised cherries, cover with a few tablespoons of kirsch and set aside.

3. Preheat oven to 190°C/375°F/Gas 5. Roll out the pastry to fit the flan tin. Grease the flan tin and line with rolled pastry.

4. To make the frangipane filling, soften the butter, add the sugar and beat until light and fluffy. Beat in the eggs a little at a time and then stir in ground almonds, flour and kirsch.

5. Place the cut cherries at the base of the flan, reserving a few for decorating. Cover with the frangipane mixture and scatter the flaked almonds on top. Bake in preheated oven for about 45 minutes.

6. Allow to cool before brushing the gâteau with glacé icing (the icing sugar mixed with hot water) and decorating with remaining cherries. Keep in a cool place in an airtight container for at least 24 hours before serving to allow the flavours to develop.

Many years ago I heard the first two lines of this prayer on the radio. As I am a lacemaker myself they meant a lot to me, so I wrote them down and have quoted them many times since. Recently I got my son to Google them and he found the rest of the prayer, which is just perfect for lacemakers and indeed all craft workers.

– Eithne Lee, Wexford

Lacemaker's Prayer

Lord, let me grow old like beautiful lace,
Cherished and treasured and cared for with grace.
Guide my hands with speed and grace
To weave the intricacies of this lace.
Let the bobbins weave with ease
To create a pattern that will please.
Let there be love in its creation
And give it artistry in its inspiration.
May special care keep the threads from breaking
And give me energy for its making.
Allow this lace to bring joy and pleasure
And give to others a lifelong treasure.

– Author unknown

Almond Tartlets

EITHNE LEE, WEXFORD

These little lacy almond tartlets can be filled with lemon curd or fresh raspberries, topped with a rosette of whipped cream and served with a lovely cup of tea in fine china set upon a lace cloth. They create the perfect excuse to take a moment to reflect on all the beautiful and precious things around us.

Makes about 12

- 50g (2oz) butter
- 50g (2oz) caster sugar
- 50g (2oz) ground almonds
- a drop of almond extract

for the filling

- lemon curd (see p127 for recipe) or fresh raspberries and freshly whipped cream

what you'll need

- shallow patty tin
- 12 paper cases (optional)
- wire rack

ICA Tip

These are flour-free tartlets, and so are suitable for coeliacs or those with a wheat intolerance.

1. Preheat oven to 180°C/350°F/Gas 4. Grease a shallow patty tin or line with paper cases.

2. Cream the butter and sugar together in a mixing bowl, and fold in the ground almonds along with a drop of almond extract. Mix well to fully incorporate.

3. Put a teaspoon of mixture in each hollow or paper case in the tin and bake in preheated oven for 20 minutes or until golden brown.

4. Allow to cool for five minutes before removing from the tin or cases and transferring to a wire rack to cool completely. If you remove them too soon, the tartlets will be too soft; if left too long, they over-harden and can be difficult to remove. Once fully cooled, store in an airtight container until ready to serve.

5. Serve with your choice of filling. I like a little lemon curd or fresh raspberries topped with a rosette of whipped cream, but these are very versatile bases, so have fun and experiment.

The Old Woman

As a white candle
In a holy place,
So is the beauty
Of an aged face.
As the spent radiance
Of the winter sun,
So is a woman
With her travail done.
Her brood gone from her
And her thoughts are still
As the waters
Under a ruined mill.

– Seosamh MacCathmhaoil (Joseph Campbell)

"No wise man ever wished to be younger."

– Jonathan Swift

"Growing old is something you do if you are lucky."

– Groucho Marx

Thursday, March 21.

"Lord, let me grow old like beautiful lace..."

Friday, March 22.

Chapter 5
Sunny Days

"Some people seemed to get all sunshine,
and some all shadow."
– Louisa May Alcott

Nobody would suggest that the Irish as a people are lucky enough to get all sunshine; some would say we hardly get our fair share of it. But there are benefits to living in a country where you may experience the gifts of four seasons in just one day. One of these benefits is that there is always the potential for things to change, for the greyness to lift and brightness to break through. And when it does, we Irish know how to make the most of it.

> "Oh, Sunlight! The most precious gold to be found on Earth."
>
> – Roman Payne

It helps that we have such a beautiful country right on our doorstep. Even our biggest cities boast magnificent hills and mountains, and breathtaking beaches and coastline within easy striking distance. It is all there for the taking: long steady hikes through fertile valleys, short family-friendly scrambles up rocky mountains, quiet meditative strolls along deserted beaches, noisy splashes in protective coves.

> "Laughter is brightest where food is best."
>
> – Irish proverb

And whether you want something sweet to give you energy for that last stretch back down the mountain or a treat to serve as part of a picnic with a flask of hot tea, or even something to return home to once appetites have been earned, there is nothing nicer than a little bit of freshly baked love to make a perfect day even better.

“That spring feeling was in the air and, after a harsh winter, there were much-needed jobs to be attended to in the garden. Having purchased early seed potatoes and onion sets, I needed to dig the vegetable patch, and the flower borders needed tidying up. I decided to recruit some family members who had flown the nest. Finally a day was arranged, with Gerald Fleming from Met Éireann promising a nice day with blue skies.

A *meitheal* of help, including grandchildren, arrived on Saturday morning. By evening time, potatoes and onions were in the soil, more ground had been prepared for vegetable seeds, and the flower borders and shrubs were looking elegant. It was time to retire to the house for a well-earned cup of tea and some home cooking. But the surprise of the evening came when 10-year-old Cormac penned a poem featuring my famous Dutch Rhubarb Cake.”

– Kay Murray, Clare

When summer comes with long fine days,
I'll be at my granny's house with friends,
having fun and playing games.

We will eat potatoes with bacon and cabbage,
and much more than we can manage,
all because of the work on this spring day,
how busy we are with forks and spades,
and still no pay.

Please God we will be here,
and remember this busy day,
with Granny and Grandad,
having orange cake and biscuits,
and that BIG POT OF TAE!

– Cormac Murray

Dutch Rhubarb Cake

KAY MURRAY, CLARE

That nice cup of tea at the end of a busy day's gardening is something special, but all the more so with something delicious to serve with it. I picked up this family favourite in North America in the 1960s.

Serves 6–8
- 285g (10oz) self-raising flour
- 85g (3oz) caster sugar
- ½ teaspoon ground cinnamon
- 85g (3oz) margarine or butter
- 150ml (¼ pint) milk
- 1 egg
- 2–3 drops vanilla extract

for the filling
- 225g (8oz) fresh rhubarb
- 1 orange, peeled of skin and pith
- 110g (4oz) caster sugar

to serve
- whipped cream or custard

what you'll need
- 28cm x 20cm (11in x 8in) Swiss roll tin

ICA Tip
This pastry is a scone mixture, so it can be doubled and used to make scones while rhubarb cake is baking. See p29 for instructions on baking scones.

1. Preheat oven to 190°C/375°F/Gas 5. Grease Swiss roll tin.

2. Sieve flour, sugar and cinnamon into a large mixing bowl, add margarine or butter and rub in with fingertips until it resembles fine breadcrumbs.

3. Beat milk and egg together until frothy, and add vanilla drops. Add most of it to mixing bowl, reserving a little to brush over the cake before baking. Work together to bind the flour into a dough, knead lightly and divide in half. Roll out one half and place into prepared Swiss roll tin. Roll out the second half.

4. Cut rhubarb into 2cm (¾in) pieces. Segment the peeled orange and roughly chop. Scatter the fruit into the Swiss roll tin, sprinkle over the sugar and cover with the second half of the dough. Brush with the reserved egg wash and bake in preheated oven for 35 minutes or until a skewer inserted into cake comes out clean.

5. Serve hot or cold with whipped cream or custard.

> " Grab your coat and get your hat
> Leave your worry on the doorstep
> Just direct your feet
> To the sunny side of the street. "

– Dorothy Fields

from Sounds of Summer

Listening to the chirping birds
Busy at their daily tasks
The leaves are whispering in the breeze
A honey bee goes buzzing past.
A tractor drones in a neighbour's field
Boasting of a busy day
Taking advantage of the sun
Cutting silage, turning hay.
A cow concerned for her calf
Calls him back with a gentle moo
The clothes are flapping on the line
Peaceful times like this are few.

– Peg Prendeville, Limerick

> " Happiness is a perfume, inside you on a shelf.
> When you sprinkle some on others,
> You spill some on yourself. "

– Elizabeth Kinnear

Courgette Cake

MAURA RIORDAN, DUBLIN

Courgette mightn't sound like an obvious ingredient for a cake, but this cake is very popular with all who have eaten it. It's also very simple to make – and perfect if you have a glut of home-grown courgettes.

Makes 900g (2lb) loaf
- 200g (7oz) courgettes, grated
- 140g (5oz) caster sugar
- 125ml (4fl oz) oil
- 1 egg
- 200g (7oz) plain flour
- ½ teaspoon bicarbonate of soda
- ¼ teaspoon baking powder
- 1 teaspoon ground cinnamon
- ½ lemon, zest only
- pinch of salt

for the icing
- 50g (2oz) cream cheese
- 25g (1oz) butter
- 140g (5oz) icing sugar

to finish
- chopped nuts or extra lemon zest

what you'll need
- 900g (2lb) loaf tin
- wire rack

1. Preheat oven to 170°C/325°F/Gas 3. Prepare loaf tin by lightly greasing or lining with baking parchment.

2. In a large mixing bowl, beat together the courgette, sugar, oil and egg. Into a separate bowl, sieve the flour, soda and baking powder, and stir in the cinnamon, zest and salt. Fold this into the courgette mixture until lightly blended and transfer into the prepared tin.

3. Bake for 45 minutes or until a skewer inserted into cake comes out clean. Allow to cool in the tin for five or ten minutes before turning out onto a wire rack to cool fully.

4. To make the icing, beat the cream cheese and butter together until light and creamy. Add the icing sugar little by little, beating until it reaches a smooth consistency. Spread over the top of the cake and finish with chopped nuts or extra lemon zest.

Like the gold of the sun,
Like the light of the day,
May the luck of the Irish
Shine bright on your way.

Like the glow of a star
And the lilt of a song,
May these be your joys
All your life long.

– Irish blessing

"Laughter is the sun that drives winter
from the human face."

– Victor Hugo

"It was only a sunny smile, and little it cost in the giving,
but like morning light it scattered the night and made
the day worth living."

– F. Scott Fitzgerald

Gingerbread

BELTRA GUILD MEMBERS, SLIGO

A slice of moist sweet gingerbread is an ideal pitstop snack during a long walk on a glorious day.

Makes 23cm (9in) loaf
- 225g (8oz) flour
- 1 tablespoon caster sugar
- ¼ teaspoon ground ginger
- ½ teaspoon mixed spice
- 85g (3oz) butter
- 3 tablespoons treacle
- 2–3 tablespoons buttermilk or sour milk
- 1 egg, beaten

what you'll need
- 23cm (9in) loaf tin

ICA Tip
You can make your own sour milk by adding a squeeze of lemon juice to some fresh milk and allowing it to acidulate for 10 minutes. Alternatively you could use sour cream or yoghurt thinned out with a little water.

1. Preheat oven to 160°C/325°F/Gas 3. Lightly grease a loaf tin.

2. Sieve the flour into a large mixing bowl and stir in the sugar and spices.

3. In a small saucepan, gently heat the butter and treacle with a little buttermilk or sour milk, taking great care not to boil the mixture. Once the butter is fully melted, allow to cool.

4. Add the beaten egg to the dry ingredients together with the butter and treacle mixture. Bind to make a very soft dough.

5. Transfer to loaf tin and bake in preheated oven for 60–90 minutes or until a skewer inserted into cake comes out clean. Check after 45 minutes, and if the cake is cooking too quickly cover the top with foil to prevent it from burning. Allow to cool fully before storing in an airtight container.

Honey Spice Cake

MARGARET SIDES, LONGFORD

Nothing quite captures the spirit of sunny days like honey, that golden gift from the industrious bees and the myriad of flowers they have visited on their travels. A variation on gingerbread, this recipe produces lighter results.

Makes about 24 squares
- 200g (7oz) self-raising flour
- 1 teaspoon mixed spice
- ½ teaspoon ground ginger
- ½ teaspoon ground cinnamon
- 140g (5oz) butter or margarine
- 110g (4oz) soft brown sugar
- 3 tablespoons honey
- 1 tablespoon water
- 2 eggs

what you'll need
- 24cm (9½in) square tin
- wire rack

1. Preheat oven to 180°C/350°F/Gas 4. Grease cake tin.

2. Sieve the flour and spices together into a large mixing bowl.

3. In a large saucepan, gently melt the butter or margarine, along with the sugar, honey and water, over a low heat, taking care not to bring to the boil. Remove from the heat and set aside to cool for 10 minutes.

4. Once fully cooled, beat the eggs into the honey mixture one at a time. Add the spiced flour and beat until thoroughly blended. Pour into prepared tin, spread evenly and bake in preheated oven for 30–35 minutes.

5. Allow to cool in the tin for 10 minutes. Carefully turn out onto a wire rack to cool fully. Once cooled, cut into squares.

Climbing Boots

Sometimes the path will turn a bend
To face a stony wall.
You see no way around it;
You climb but then you fall.
Look up my friend and over,
These boots will help you on,
Just turn your face to Heaven –
A new path has begun.

– Author unknown

"Never let the sun go down on your anger."

– Proverb

"Bitterness imprisons life;
Love releases it."

– Harry Emerson Fosdick

Baked Cherry Cheesecake

MAURA RIORDAN, DUBLIN

With the use of a blender to whip up the ingredients before baking, this really is such an easy recipe to pull together with minimal effort and maximum results. Your waistline will thank you for using cottage cheese in place of richer cream cheese too.

Serves 8

- 200g (7oz) wholegrain biscuits
- 100g (3½oz) butter or margarine, room temperature
- 450g (1lb) cottage cheese
- 570ml (1 pint) milk
- 140g (5oz) sugar
- 2 tablespoons plain flour
- ¼ teaspoon salt
- 4 large eggs
- 1 teaspoon lemon juice

to finish

- 1 large tin of cherry pie filling

what you'll need

- 20cm (8in) loose-bottomed cake tin
- blender

1. Preheat oven to 170°C/325°F/Gas 3. Lightly grease the cake tin.

2. Crush biscuits in a mixing bowl and mix with softened butter until well combined. Line the base of the cake tin with this biscuit mixture and set aside.

3. In a blender, combine the cottage cheese, milk, sugar, flour, salt, eggs and lemon juice, and blitz until smooth. Pour over biscuit base and bake in preheated oven for 60–90 minutes or until set.

4. Remove from oven and allow to cool for 10 minutes before carefully detaching the base of the tin from the ring. Allow to cool fully and top with cherry pie filling.

Curd Cheesecake

LIZ WALL, WICKLOW

Curd cheese is lower in fat, lighter in texture and higher in acidity than ordinary cream cheese. It makes for a lighter, healthier and tangier style of cheesecake.

Serves 8
- shortcrust pastry (shop bought or see recipe on p153: freeze any leftover pastry)
- 4 eggs, separated
- 175g (6oz) caster sugar
- 150ml (¼ pint) single cream
- 1 lemon, juice and rind
- 1 tablespoon cornflour
- 450g (1lb) curd cheese
- 50g (2oz) sultanas

what you'll need
- 23cm (9in) loose-bottomed cake tin
- baking beans

ICA Tip
If you can't source curd cheese, you could use cottage cheese that has been well drained and blitzed to a smooth paste.

1. Preheat oven to 190°C/375°F/Gas 5 and lightly grease the base of the loose-bottomed cake tin.

2. Roll out the pastry and transfer it to line the base of the cake tin. Blind bake for 10 minutes using dried baking beans to weigh the pastry down. Remove from oven and set aside to cool. Reduce oven to 170°C/325°F/Gas 3.

3. In a large mixing bowl, beat together the egg yolks with the sugar and add the cream, lemon juice, lemon rind and cornflour. Stir in the curd cheese and sultanas. In a clean bowl, whisk the egg whites until stiff and fold into the cheese mixture.

4. Pour onto the pastry base and cook in the middle of the oven for about 60 minutes, or until cake is brown on top and firm to the touch. Allow to cool fully before carefully removing from tin.

Moist Almond Slices

WINNIE McCARRON, MONAGHAN

I have been making this simple traybake for a long number of years. It's versatile (you can swap the jam for mincemeat at Christmas), keeps well and is quick to make, especially if you have the pastry already made and stored in the freezer. Perfect as a tasty snack in a picnic lunch.

Serves 6–8

- 2 tablespoons raspberry or strawberry jam
- 3–4 handfuls almond flakes

for the pastry

- 170g (6oz) plain flour
- 110g (4oz) butter
- 1–2 tablespoons ice-cold water

for the topping

- 225g (8oz) butter
- 225g (8oz) caster sugar
- 50g (2oz) ground almonds
- 170g (6oz) ground rice
- 2 eggs
- 2 teaspoons almond extract

what you'll need

- 28cm x 20cm (11in x 8in) Swiss roll tin

ICA Tip

If you prefer a sweet pastry you could add a dessertspoon of sugar to the pastry mix, but the filling should make this sweet enough. This pastry freezes well.

1. Preheat oven to 170°C/325°F/Gas 3. Lightly grease Swiss roll tin.

2. To make the pastry, in a large mixing bowl mix the flour and butter together with your fingertips until it resembles fine breadcrumbs. Incorporate as much air as possible into the mixture by raising your hands in the air and letting the mixture fall into the bowl slowly. Add the water and bind the pastry with a knife until it comes together. Refrigerate for 20 minutes to rest.

3. To make the almond topping, melt butter in a saucepan. Allow to cool before adding sugar, ground almonds and ground rice, stirring to mix well. Beat the eggs and almond extract together and add to mixture.

4. On a lightly floured board, roll pastry out into a rectangle large enough to fit your Swiss roll tin. Carefully transfer pastry to tin and top with a light spread of jam. Pour the topping over the base and scatter with flaked almonds.

5. Bake in preheated oven for 35–40 minutes or until the mixture is pale and golden. Allow to cool and cut into slices to enjoy immediately or store in an airtight container.

from The Wind that Shakes the Barley

Above the uplands drenched with dew
The sky hangs soft and pearly,
An emerald world is listening to
The wind that shakes the barley.

...

Oh, still through summers and through springs
It calls me late and early.
Come home, come home, come home, it sings,
The wind that shakes the barley.

– Katharine Tynan

from The Daffodils

I wandered lonely as a cloud
That floats on high o'er vales and hills,
When all at once I saw a crowd,
A host, of golden daffodils.

...

I gazed – and gazed – but little thought
What wealth the show to me had brought:

For oft, when on my couch I lie
In vacant or in pensive mood,
They flash upon that inward eye
Which is the bliss of solitude;
And then my heart with pleasure fills,
And dances with the daffodils.

– William Wordsworth

... direct your feet to the Sunny side of the Street.

Chapter 6
Rainy Days

"Every cloud has a silver lining."
– Proverb

Ireland really does get more than its fair share of rain – although, as any Irish person can tell you, there's a difference between a proper rainy day and all of those other days during which it may well rain. Drizzly days or soft days, spitty days or low-cloud days – none of these really count as truly rainy days. To qualify, a day needs to have a downpour or deluge, and the rain has to be absolutely lashing, pounding the pavements, driving at the window sideways or bucketing down from the heavens. Thankfully, even rainy days bring their several blessings. We don't get our 40 shades of green without sacrificing a little blue sky. And those green fields and the fine dairy cattle they feed give us the world-class milk and butter that puts our home baking among the best in the world.

"A negative mind will never give you a positive life."

– Anonymous

Our fickle weather also encourages spontaneity in our national character. We have to be ready to change our plans according to the plans the heavens have in store for us. That sometimes means postponing leaving the house until a squall passes, and passing the time with a chat over tea and biscuits; or, if the wet skies are settling in, surrendering to a day indoors spent curled up with a book or battling over board games. On rainy days like these, what a pleasure it is to know that we have fuel on hand to light the fire, and enough store-cupboard essentials to whip up some home-baked goodies to bring a little sunshine back into our day. Besides, imagine how dull life would be if there were no seasons to mark the passing of time and no mercurial weather to surprise us. Thank the Lord for the rain.

"People don't notice whether it's winter or summer when they're happy."

– Anton Chekhov

" I know that many people make more complaints about rainy days than any other, but I love the sound of rain in all its forms and I don't understand why it gets such a bad rap.

On rainy days when I was a child, the workman who brought the milk in would always say to my mother "Grand soft day, mam", whether there was a mist or a downpour, hailstones or that beautiful gentle rain you get in the west, and as a child I never really realised how right he was.

For me rainy days are an inspiration, in many ways. They mean that I don't need to go out and get wet and cold, but can take my book and curl up on the couch, ignore the weather and enjoy a steaming mug of tea and biscuits. I can put off those tasks that I don't want to do anyway.

If I have to go out then I am lucky to have a car and a warm coat to get around in. And it gives me the opportunity to watch the children who love to jump in puddles, despite being told off about getting wet or splashing others. It doesn't matter to them; they are filled with the joy of life. They remind me of my childhood, when one of the most fun things we did was to go to the bog with my father and mess around. The sensation of squishy wet turf between the toes and the taste of sweet tea from a can have proven to be unforgettable. "

– Anne Payne, Laois

" Raindrops filter through leaves, silver the air,
Wash off the film of dust to release nets
Of fragrance on which the wind can sweeten... "

– John O'Donohue

Tea Brack

TERESA DOONER, LONGFORD

A thick slice of tea brack (or breac) spread with cold farmhouse butter and served with hot tea is one of Irish life's most treasured pleasures. Don't be afraid to spread that butter thick – the brack is baked without any butter or margarine to begin with (one of the reasons it keeps so well).

Makes two 900g (2lb) loaves
- 375g (13oz) mixed dried fruit
- 570ml (1 pint) cold tea
- 450g (1lb) self-raising flour
- 225g (8oz) caster sugar
- pinch of mixed spice
- pinch of ground nutmeg
- 2 eggs, beaten

what you'll need
- 2 x 900g (2lb) loaf tins
- wire rack

ICA Tip
Storing the well-wrapped cake for a couple of days before serving will allow the flavours to develop more fully.

1. In a large mixing bowl, combine fruit and cold tea and leave to soak overnight.

2. Preheat oven to 170°C/325°F/Gas 3. Grease two loaf tins.

3. Sieve the flour and sugar into the bowl of soaked fruit. Add the spices and beaten eggs and mix well.

4. Transfer into prepared tins and bake in preheated oven for about 60 minutes, or until a skewer inserted into cake comes out clean. Transfer to a wire rack to cool fully. Wrap in baking parchment and store in an airtight container where they will keep for at least two weeks.

" When anyone asks me about the Irish character,
I say look at the trees. Maimed, stark and misshapen,
but ferociously tenacious. "

– Edna O'Brien

" In Ireland you go to someone's house and she asks you if you want a cup of tea. You say no, thank you, you're really just fine. She asks if you're SURE. You say of course you're sure. Really you don't need a thing. Except they pronounce it TING. You don't need a ting. Well, she says then, I was going to get myself some anyway, so it would be no trouble. Ah, you say, well if you were going to get yourself some I wouldn't mind a spot of tea at that so long as it's no trouble and I can give you a hand in the kitchen. Then you go through the whole thing all over again until you both end up in the kitchen drinking tea and chatting.

In America someone asks you if you want a cup of tea,
you say no, and then you don't get any damned tea!
I liked the Irish way better. "

– from *Urban Shaman* by C.E. Murphy

" Come and share a pot of tea,
my home is warm and my friendship's free. "

– Emilie Barnes

" Generosity is giving more than you can,
and pride is taking less than you need. "

– Kahlil Gibran

Almond Biscuits

BETTY GORMAN, LAOIS

In my book, there's nothing quite like a cup of tea and a homemade almond biscuit. These are easy to make and keep for ages, so you need never go without them.

Makes 24 biscuits
- 225g (8oz) moist brown sugar
- 225g (8oz) butter
- ½ teaspoon almond extract
- 2 eggs, beaten
- 350g (12oz) plain flour
- 1 teaspoon baking powder
- 225g (8oz) ground almonds

what you'll need
- biscuit cutter
- baking tray or sheet
- wire rack

1. Preheat oven to 180°C/350°F/Gas 4. Line a baking tray or sheet with baking parchment.

2. In a large saucepan, melt butter and sugar together over a gentle heat, taking care not to allow the mixture to boil.

3. Transfer to a large mixing bowl and allow to cool a little. Add almond extract and beaten eggs, and stir to mix. Sieve in the flour and baking powder together, add the almonds and stir to integrate into a soft dough.

4. Transfer the dough to a lightly floured surface and roll out to about ½cm (¼in) thickness. Cut out shapes with biscuit cutter and place on lined baking tray.

5. Bake in preheated oven for 15 minutes or until lightly golden. Allow to cool on a wire rack and store in an airtight container, where they will keep for up to two weeks.

Quarkblätterteig

MAURA RIORDAN, DUBLIN

This unusual recipe was given to me by a German lady, Gisela O'Connor, who lived in Ireland for many years and who served as secretary of the Castlebar Song Contest until it ceased to take place. They look very delicate and pretty when piled on a plate for serving.

Makes about 48

- 225g (8oz) plain flour
- 3 teaspoons baking powder
- 225g (8oz) cottage cheese, drained of excess liquid
- 225g (8oz) cold margarine, cut into pieces
- 3–4 drops vanilla extract (optional)

for the filling

- lemon curd (shop bought or see p127 for recipe)

for the icing

- 200g icing sugar
- 2 tablespoons water, just boiled

what you'll need

- baking tray or sheet
- wire rack

ICA Tip

You can vary the filling in these, experimenting with homemade fruit jam or even omitting the vanilla extract and icing and using savoury fillings such as mushroom pâté.

1. Preheat oven to 180°C/350°F/Gas 4.

2. Sieve flour and baking powder into a large mixing bowl. Make a hole in the middle and add cottage cheese, margarine and vanilla. Cover margarine with flour and beat everything together to a smooth dough.

3. Roll out very thinly on a lightly floured surface, fold over several times and roll out a little before wrapping in cling film and refrigerating overnight.

4. Roll out very thinly into a large square or rectangle. Cut into 6cm (2½in) squares. Place a little lemon curd in the middle of each and fold over into a mixture of triangles and rectangles, pressing the edges to seal.

5. Pour a little water over a baking tray or sheet and pour off without wiping. Place the filled shapes onto the tray and bake in preheated oven for about 10–15 minutes or until golden brown.

6. Transfer to a wire rack. Thin out icing sugar with enough hot water to make it spreadable, and spread over the quarkblätterteig while still hot. Allow to cool to set the icing and pile onto a serving plate to serve.

Lemon Curd

SALLY DUNLEAVY, MAYO

This delicious recipe came to me from my late mother-in-law, Mrs Peg Dunleavy. It makes for a lovely gift to bring to a friend, maybe with some homemade scones, or can be used to top a lemon cake (see p128 or p131) or to sandwich two layers. Children love it simply spread on bread.

Makes about 3–4 small jars

- 85g (3oz) butter
- 450g (1lb) sugar
- 4 unwaxed lemons, juice and zest
- 6 eggs, beaten

what you'll need

- 4–5 jars, sterilised (see p30 for instructions)
- baking parchment
- string or rubber bands
- labels

ICA Tip

Always use unwaxed lemons in recipes where the zest or grated rind is called for. But if you can't find any, give ordinary waxed lemons a scrub in hot water to remove the wax.

1. Melt the butter in a clean non-aluminium saucepan over a gentle heat. Add the sugar, lemon juice and lemon zest, and stir to mix well.

2. Add in the beaten eggs and continue to cook slowly, stirring over a very gentle heat until it thickens. If it looks like the edges are about to bubble at any point, remove from the heat and continue to stir until it thickens. (If you prefer, you can cook this over a bain-marie to avoid it curdling. See p193.)

3. Transfer to sterilised glass jars, cover with baking parchment and secure with string or rubber bands. Label with date and name. Store in the fridge until ready to use, where it will keep for up to a week.

Lemon Cake

BREDA BROWN, KERRY

*What is better than lemon cake for bringing a little sunshine back into your day?
The beauty of this recipe is its simplicity. Orange cake can be made in the same way:
simply substitute grated orange rind and juice for the lemon.*

Serves 6–8

- 285g (10oz) self-raising flour
- 225g (8oz) soft butter or margarine
- 225g (8oz) caster sugar
- 2 teaspoons baking powder
- 2 lemons, zest only
- 4 dessertspoons milk
- 4 eggs

for the icing

- 225g (8oz) icing sugar
- 3 tablespoons lemon juice

what you'll need

- 23cm x 28cm (9in x 11in) cake tin

ICA Tip

This all-in-one method is great for producing buns and cupcakes too – you could replace the milk with water for a lighter result.

1. Preheat oven to 180°C/350°F/Gas 4. Line cake tin with baking parchment.

2. Using the all-in-one method, combine all ingredients in a large mixing bowl and beat together with an electric whisk for about a minute, starting at a slow speed and increasing the speed as the ingredients come together.

3. Pour into lined tin and bake in preheated oven for 35–40 minutes, or until a skewer inserted into cake comes out clean.

4. Allow to cool before removing from the tin. Mix the icing sugar with enough lemon juice to produce an icing of runny consistency. Once the cake is cool, remove from tin and cover with icing. Allow to set.

My house is small,
No mansion for a millionaire,
But there is room for love
And there is room for friends –
That's all I care.

– Author unknown

"Happiness does not come from having
much but from being attached to little."

– Anonymous

"Grant me a sense of humour, Lord,
The saving grace to see a joke,
To win some happiness from life,
And pass it on to other folk."

– Author unknown

Citrus Poppy Seed Cake

AN GRIANÁN, LOUTH

This alternative citrus cake recipe is a little more complex than the previous version (see p128), but the inclusion of yoghurt makes it a moister cake, so it will keep well if stored in an airtight container.

Serves 6–8

- 250g (9oz) self-raising flour
- 175g (6oz) soft margarine
- 175g (6oz) caster sugar
- 50g (2oz) poppy seeds
- 4 generous tablespoons yoghurt
- 2 oranges, zest only
- 2 lemons, zest only
- 3 eggs

for the icing

- 3 tablespoons lemon curd (shop bought or see p127 for recipe)
- 1 tablespoon orange juice
- 110g (4oz) cream cheese

what you'll need

- 20cm (8in) cake tin

1. Preheat oven to 170°C/325°F/Gas 3. Line cake tin with baking parchment.

2. Using the all-in-one method, combine all ingredients in a large mixing bowl and beat together with an electric whisk for about a minute, starting at a slow speed and increasing the speed as the ingredients come together.

3. Spread mixture into lined tin and bake in preheated oven for 45 minutes, or until a skewer inserted into cake comes out clean. Cool for 10 minutes in tin.

4. Meanwhile, beat the ingredients for the icing together and place in fridge until cake is fully cooled. Spread icing over cake and serve, or wrap in baking parchment and store in an airtight container until ready to serve.

from Just a Little Hug

When the sun is refusing
to shine on your day
and you're finding it hard
just to cope,
When you're seeing more rain clouds
than stars in the sky
and you just feel like giving up hope,
That's the time when someone
comes along with a smile
and a warm hug
that says, "It's okay –
Tomorrow is coming,
so don't give up now,
brighter moments are soon on their way!"

– Emily Matthews

Cheat's Passion Fruit & Lime Soufflé

AN GRIANÁN, LOUTH

This cheat's soufflé couldn't be simpler and will bring some instant sunshine to any rainy day. Most shop-bought custard has a good shelf life and both limes and passion fruit last well, making this something you can whip together with minimal notice.

Serves 4–6

- 400ml (14fl oz) custard, shop bought or see p147 for recipe
- 3 tablespoons icing sugar
- 2 limes, grated rind only
- 3 ripe passion fruit
- 3 egg whites
- 1 tablespoon caster sugar

what you'll need

- ovenproof soufflé dish

ICA Tip

Use reduced-fat ready-made custard if you'd prefer to keep this treat guilt free.

1. Preheat oven to 190°C/375°F/Gas 5 and preheat the grill to medium.

2. Place the custard in a large mixing bowl and stir in the icing sugar, grated lime rind and passion fruit pulp and seeds.

3. In a separate bowl, whisk the egg whites until stiff. Using a large metal spoon, gently fold the egg whites into the custard mixture.

4. Carefully transfer the mixture to a large ovenproof soufflé dish, level off the surface and sprinkle with caster sugar.

5. Pop the soufflé under preheated grill for three minutes to melt the sugar. Transfer to preheated oven and bake for 20 minutes until well risen and set. Serve immediately.

Mango Cheesecake

AN GRIANÁN, LOUTH

Nothing says sunshine like the vibrant colour and sweet tang of mango, and this clever cheesecake captures all of that on a plate – just the thing to banish the rainy-day blues.

Serves 6–8
- 350g (12oz) Polo biscuits
- 160g (5½oz) butter, melted
- 250g (9oz) Philadelphia Cream Cheese
- 100g (3½oz) caster sugar
- 2 teaspoons vanilla extract
- 150ml (¼ pint) milk
- 4 gelatine leaves
- 275ml (½ pint) cream, whipped
- 1 packet lemon jelly
- 300ml (10fl oz) mango coulis, shop bought or see tip below

what you'll need
- 30cm (12in) loose-bottomed flan tin

ICA Tip
If you can't find shop-bought mango coulis, you could thicken a 300ml Innocent mango and passion fruit smoothie with two teaspoons of cornflour.

1. Break up the biscuits into a mixing bowl and mix in melted butter until well integrated. Press into base of flan tin and set aside.

2. Cream together the cheese and sugar. Add vanilla and mix well. Warm the milk gently in a small saucepan, then add the gelatine and allow to fully dissolve. Cool a little before adding to cheese mixture.

3. Whip the cream until it forms soft peaks. Fold this into the cheese mixture, then transfer the mixture onto the biscuit base and allow to set (about 20 minutes).

4. Prepare the jelly according to the packet instructions. Add the mango coulis to the jelly and pour the mixture over the set cheesecake. Allow jelly to set before gently removing from cake tin and serving.

from A Burren Prayer

May the praise of rain on stone,
Recall the child lost in the heart's catacomb.

May the light that turns the limestone white
Remind us that our solitude is bright.

May the arrival of gentians in their blue surprise
Bring glimpses of delight to our eyes.

May the wells that dream in the stone
Soothe the eternal that sleeps in our bone.

– John O'Donohue

“ The drop of rain maketh a hole in the stone,
not by violence, but by oft falling. ”

– Hugh Latimer

EVERY CLOUD HAS A SILVER LINING

Chapter 7
Festive Days

"Thank you for the days,
Those endless days, those sacred days you gave me."
– The Kinks

We Irish have always had a fondness for festivities, and communal celebrations or festivals have long been central to our society. Many of today's festivals and feast days revolve around the Christian calendar, but often these are infused with the remnants of ancient pagan rituals and Celtic thanksgiving festivals marking the changing of the seasons. And so on 1 February we celebrate St Brigid's Day – the patron saint of students, farmers and artists – which coincides with the Celtic festival of Imbolc, marking the first day of spring and the start of the farming year. Easter remembers the resurrection of Christ, but is also connected with the pagan cult of the Saxon goddess of spring, Éostre. Fires are lit on the hills on May Day to celebrate the return of Bealtaine, or the beginning of summer, and again on St John's Day which (almost) coincides with the summer solstice or Midsummer's Eve. Halloween brings together the Christian All Saints' Day and the pagan harvest celebrations of Samhain.

> **Let us break bread together...**
> **Let us drink wine together...**
> **Let us praise God together.**

– Traditional Christian hymn

Many of the traditions and rituals surrounding these festivals centre on the preparing and sharing of food. In the lead-up to Easter, the Christian practice of Lenten abstinence remains a strong tradition, and much of the food eaten on Good Friday and Easter Sunday is imbued with religious symbolism. Christmas is a very special time for us Irish, when the celebration of Christ's birth in a manger reminds us how lucky we are to have shelter for our own families, many of whom return from all over the world for this annual family reunion. Each of these many festive days reminds us to give thanks for all that we have.

> **Always remember to forget the things that made you sad.**
> **But never forget to remember the things that made you glad.**

– Anonymous

> **"Bread and water can so easily be toast and tea."**
>
> – Anonymous

> **"**Growing up in rural Ireland in the 1950s, we didn't have many parties. But on Easter Sunday we had what we then referred to as a feast. On that special occasion we joined with neighbouring families and celebrated in style!
>
> Early in the afternoon my father lit a fire in a sheltered part of the small field (or paddock as we call it now) near the house. We boiled a pot of eggs, followed by a kettle of water for tea, and laid out the rest of the goodies for the feast on an old sheet.
>
> We had cup cakes, rock buns and another cake which we called a 'sliotar', which was really a sponge cake without a filling. It was delicious. We also had 'Easter eggs', which were small marshmallows covered in chocolate. (We hadn't seen large eggs in boxes at that stage, except in shop windows.) During Lent we children always fasted from sweets and saved any we got in a shoebox stored on top of the wardrobe. There would be a great variety in that box – Scots Clan, Emeralds, Double Centres, bull's eyes, Peggy's Legs – all to be enjoyed during the feast.
>
> This day was regarded as the beginning of summer, and so we wore our ankle socks for the first time that year. We were probably covered in goose bumps, but we didn't care. After we had eaten our fill, we played chasing or hide and seek.
>
> By six or seven in the evening, we would be exhausted and our visitors would depart for their own homes. It was a magical day for us. I am so grateful to my father for starting this annual event in our community and giving us so many wonderful childhood memories.**"**
>
> – Emily McCarthy, Dublin

> **"Everything in moderation, including moderation."**
>
> – Oscar Wilde

Orange & Cinnamon Hot Cross Buns

EDWARD HAYDEN, ICA COOKERY TUTOR

Since the seventeenth century, hot cross buns have been baked and eaten on Good Friday to remind us of the sufferings of Jesus on the cross. This traditional recipe is simpler than it looks – take your time and success will be yours.

Makes 12 buns
- 300g (10oz) strong baker's flour
- 1 teaspoon ground cinnamon
- ½ teaspoon ground nutmeg
- pinch of salt
- 1 orange, grated zest only
- 50g (2oz) butter
- 50g (2oz) brown sugar
- 200g (7oz) sultanas
- 2 egg yolks

for the batter
- 110g (4oz) strong baker's flour
- 1 dessertspoon light brown sugar
- 1 x 7g sachet easy-blend dried yeast
- 250ml (9fl oz) warm milk

for the cross
- 2 tablespoons plain flour
- a little water

for the orange & cinnamon glaze
- 85g (3oz) caster sugar
- 1 orange, juice only
- 1 cinnamon stick
- 100ml (3½fl oz) water

what you'll need
- baking sheet
- piping bag

1. Preheat oven to 190°C/375°F/Gas 5 and lightly grease a flat baking sheet.

2. Combine the batter ingredients and mix together well. Transfer to a large mixing bowl to give the mixture room to rise and swell. Cover with cling film and set aside for 30 minutes or until the mixture has bubbled up and become frothy.

3. Meanwhile, to make the dough, sieve the flour, spices and salt into a large mixing bowl. Add in the orange zest and butter, rubbing the butter into the dry ingredients until they resemble breadcrumbs. Stir in the sugar and sultanas.

4. Pour the batter in on top of the dry ingredients. Beat two egg yolks with a tablespoon of water and add for extra richness. Mix until all of the ingredients have come together. Transfer to a lightly floured surface and knead for four to five minutes.

5. Divide dough into 12 balls and place them side by side on prepared baking sheet, leaving a little room between each as they will spread. Cover with a dry cloth and leave to rise in a warm environment for about an hour.

6. When the rolls have almost doubled in size, blend a little flour and water into a paste and pipe a cross on top of each bun. Bake in preheated oven for 20 minutes until golden brown.

7. Meanwhile, combine the glaze ingredients in a saucepan and bring to the boil. Reduce for three or four minutes until a thick syrup has been achieved. Brush the top of the baked buns with the boiling syrup and allow to cool before serving.

143

Simnel Cake

ANNE PAYNE, LAOIS

A light fruit cake baked at Easter time with a central layer of almond paste for added moisture, simnel cake has a traditional decoration of 12 balls of almond paste to represent Jesus and his eleven true apostles, leaving Judas to his own fate.

Serves 12–15

- 250g (9oz) unsalted butter
- 200g (7oz) brown sugar
- 4 eggs
- 250g (9oz) plain flour
- 1 teaspoon baking powder
- 1 teaspoon mixed spice
- 250g (9oz) raisins, chopped coarsely
- 150g (5½oz) sultanas
- 50g (2oz) mixed peel
- 600g almond paste (ready-made or see p146 for recipe)
- 4 tablespoons apricot jam

to decorate (optional)

- mini eggs or chicks
- sugared flowers
- ribbon

what you'll need

- 25cm (10in) loose-bottomed cake tin

1. Preheat oven to 180°C/350°F/Gas 4. Grease the tin and line with baking parchment.

2. Beat butter and sugar until light and creamy. Beat in eggs one at a time, incorporating each before adding the next.

3. Sieve in the flour, baking powder and mixed spice, and fold in to incorporate. Fold through dried fruit, stirring well to mix, and spoon half of the mixture into the prepared cake tin, levelling it out.

4. Divide the almond paste in three. Roll out one third into a 25cm (10in) circle. Place over the fruit mixture. Pour remaining mixture on top and bake for 90 minutes or until a skewer inserted into cake comes out clean. Check the cake after 30 minutes; if it is browning too quickly, loosely cover with tin foil. Once cooked, allow cake to cool completely before removing from tin.

5. Meanwhile, roll out another third of the almond paste into a 25cm (10in) circle. Loosen the apricot jam with a little boiling water to make a glaze and brush this over the cooled cake. Top with the almond paste circle and trim to fit.

6. Divide the remaining almond paste in thirds, quarter each third and roll into 12 balls. Place these on top of the cake and flash under a hot grill for three minutes or until golden brown. Decorate as desired.

Almond Paste

EDWARD HAYDEN, ICA COOKERY TUTOR

You can buy almond paste (or marzipan), but if you make your own you will taste the difference.

Makes enough for three 25cm (10in) discs

- 285g (10oz) ground almonds
- 140g (5oz) icing sugar
- 140g (5oz) caster sugar
- 1 large egg
- ½ teaspoon almond essence
- ½ lemon, juice only

ICA Tip

If you make the almond paste in advance, take it out of the fridge about 30 minutes before you need it to ensure it is soft enough to roll out.

1. Sieve the ground almonds and icing sugar together into a bowl. Add the caster sugar and mix well.

2. In a separate bowl, whisk the egg, almond essence and lemon juice with a fork.

3. Add two thirds of this liquid to the dry ingredients and bind them together. Do not add all of the liquid at once as you may not need it all, depending on the size of your egg. Add the remaining third of the liquid only if it is needed to bind the mixture together. Use a little cold water if extra liquid is needed. The almond paste should look like a ball of pastry after it has been kneaded together.

4. Divide the paste into three lots, wrap each in cling film and store in the fridge until required.

Homemade Custard

AN GRIANÁN, LOUTH

Homemade custard is worth the effort, especially if you use a real vanilla pod in place of synthetic flavourings. Custard freezes well, so consider making a double batch and freezing what you don't use.

Makes about 850ml (1½ pints)
- 200ml (7fl oz) double cream
- 700ml (1¼ pints) milk
- 1 vanilla pod
- 4 egg yolks
- 3 tablespoons cornflour
- 170g (6oz) caster sugar

ICA Tip
If you see any lumps forming while you're thickening the custard, remove from the heat immediately and don't cook it any further.

1. Combine the cream and milk in a large pan over a gentle heat. Scrape in the vanilla seeds and add the pod. Bring to a slow simmer.

2. Meanwhile, whisk the egg yolks, cornflour and sugar together in a large mixing bowl. Gradually pour in the hot milk mixture, whisking constantly.

3. Rinse and dry the saucepan and return the combined mixture to it. Reheat gently, stirring with a wooden spoon until it thickens. Remove the vanilla pod and serve hot or cold.

> "When fruit has ripened on the tree
> And grain is gathered from the field,
> We place our offerings in the church
> In thanks for one more season's yield."
>
> – Francis Gay

> "When the apple is ripe it will fall."
>
> – Irish proverb

> "Too much of a good thing can be wonderful."
>
> – Mae West

Mid-Western Apple Cake

MARY FITZGERALD, WEXFORD

This crowd-friendly recipe is perfect for celebrating the Lughnasa (harvest time) festival. It takes about five minutes to throw together and cooks in an ordinary roasting pan, so you get plenty for very little effort.

Serves 12–14

- 4 medium-sized cooking apples, peeled and diced small
- 200g (7oz) caster sugar
- 125g (4½oz) plain flour
- ½ teaspoon ground cinnamon
- 1 teaspoon bread soda
- 2 eggs, well beaten
- 275ml (½ pint) sunflower or vegetable oil
- 140g (5oz) chopped nuts (optional)

what you'll need

- 23cm x 30cm (9in x 12in) roasting pan

1. Preheat oven to 190°C/375°F/Gas 5. Lightly grease and flour a roasting pan.

2. Combine all ingredients in a large mixing bowl and mix well. Pour into prepared roasting pan and bake in preheated oven for 50–60 minutes or until a skewer inserted into cake comes out clean.

3. Serve warm with custard or ice-cream, or allow to cool in the pan and cut into squares to store in an airtight container.

"Pumpkins are traditionally eaten in the United States at Halloween but have become popular in Ireland. The original jack-o'-lantern was actually a turnip and the tradition is based on an old Irish legend.

Jack lured the devil up a tree to get an apple and marked the tree with the sign of the cross to prevent the devil from coming down again. When Jack died he was not allowed into heaven because of his drunken ways and so he went down to hell instead. But the devil remembered him and turned him away, throwing a hot coal at him as he did so. Jack was eating a turnip at the time, which was hit by the coal. Poor Jack has wandered the earth with his jack-o'-lantern ever since, seeking a place to rest."

– Maura Riordan, Dublin

It's late and we are sleepy, the air is cold and still,
Our jack-o'-lantern grins at us upon the window sill.
We're stuffed with cake and candy, and we've had lots of fun,
But now it's time to go to bed and dream of all we've done.
We'll dream of ghosts and goblins and of witches that we've seen,
And we'll dream of trick or treating on this happy Halloween.

– Author unknown

Pumpkin Pie

MAURA RIORDAN, DUBLIN

Halloween has roots in the Irish pagan festival Samhain, and we Irish brought it to the rest of the world by way of North America. But traditions have travelled both ways, and pumpkins, which are traditionally eaten in the United States at Halloween, have become popular in Ireland, both to carve for decoration and to eat.

Serves 8–10
- 250g (8oz) plain flour
- 110g (4oz) butter, cubed
- 3–4 tablespoons cold water
- 1kg (2lb) pumpkin flesh
- 100g (3½oz) brown sugar
- 1 teaspoon ground cinnamon
- 1 teaspoon ground ginger
- 1 teaspoon grated nutmeg
- 3 eggs, beaten
- 300ml (10fl oz) cream, whipped

what you'll need
- 28cm (11in) loose-bottomed flan tin
- baking beans

1. In a bowl, mix the flour and butter together with your fingertips until it resembles fine breadcrumbs. Incorporate as much air as possible into the mixture by raising your hands in the air and letting the mixture fall into the bowl slowly. Add the water and bind the pastry with a knife until it comes together.

2. Cook the chopped pumpkin flesh with a little water in a tightly covered saucepan for about 20 minutes or until soft. Mash well and leave to cool.

3. Meanwhile, grease the flan tin. Roll out the pastry on a lightly floured surface to fit the base and sides of the tin. Line the tin with the pastry and refrigerate for 30 minutes. Preheat oven to 200°C/400°F/Gas 6.

4. Once the pastry has rested, pour in some baking beans to weigh the pastry down and bake blind for about 20 minutes. Remove the baking beans and allow the pastry to cool a little.

5. Mix sugar and spices, and add to the beaten eggs. Fold in the cooled pumpkin and whipped cream. Mix well and pour into the pastry case.

6. Bake in preheated for about 50 minutes or until set. Serve hot or cold.

The Woodcarver

———— • ————

In these days of mass production, cheap and shoddy fake,
It is good to come across a craftsman who can make
Lovely things that grow in beauty as the years pass by,
Satisfying to the mind and pleasing to the eye.

– Patience Strong

Christmas Tree Blessing

———— • ————

Holy Creator of Trees, bless with your abundant grace
this, our Christmas tree, as a symbol of joy.
May its evergreen branches be a sign of your never-fading promises.
May its colourful lights and ornaments call us to decorate with love
our home and our world.
May the gifts that surround this tree be symbols of the gifts
we have received from the Tree of Christ's Cross.
Holy Christmas tree within our home,
may Joy and Peace come and nest in your branches and in our hearts.
Amen.

– Author unknown

Cut-before-Christmas Cranberry Cake

BREDA BROWN, KERRY

The cranberries in this cake help to keep it nice and moist. It can be served within a week of baking and will keep well for several weeks, if it's not eaten before then.

Makes one 23cm (9in) cake
- 450g (1lb) raisins
- 340g (12oz) sultanas
- 110g (4oz) dried peel
- 110g (4oz) glacé cherries
- 110g (4oz) cranberries (fresh or frozen)
- 5 dessertspoons brandy
- 285g (10oz) butter
- 285g (10oz) brown sugar
- 340g (12oz) plain flour
- 1 teaspoon ground cinnamon
- 1 teaspoon allspice
- 5 eggs
- 1 orange, zest only
- 1 lemon, zest only
- 110g (4oz) ground almonds
- 110g (4oz) flaked almonds

what you'll need
- 23cm (9in) cake tin

1. In a covered bowl, soak the dried fruit in the brandy overnight.

2. Preheat oven to 150°C/300°F/Gas 2. Line cake tin with baking parchment.

3. In a large mixing bowl, beat butter and sugar together until light and fluffy. In a separate bowl, sieve together the flour and spices.

4. Little by little, incorporate the eggs and the combined flour and spices into the butter and sugar mix, adding an egg, then some flour, and continuing until all of the flour and eggs are incorporated.

5. Stir in the soaked fruit, citrus zest and almonds. Mix well and pour into lined cake tin. Bake in preheated oven for 60 minutes. Reduce oven heat to 130°C/250°F/Gas ½ and bake for a further 90 minutes, but keep a close eye on the cake as oven temperatures vary. It is ready when a skewer inserted into cake comes out clean.

6. Allow to cool in the tin before transferring to an airtight container and storing for at least a week before serving. It will keep well for two to three weeks.

156

Cranberry Mousse

MAURA RIORDAN, DUBLIN

Don't tell Granny, but the truth is that not everyone loves a traditional Christmas pudding. This Finnish recipe makes a great festive alternative.

Serves 10
- 175g (6oz) caster sugar
- 600ml (1 pint) water
- 450g (1lb) cranberries
- 1 lemon, juice only
- 1 orange, juice only
- 5 teaspoons powdered gelatine
- 5 tablespoons hot water
- 600ml (1 pint) double cream

what you'll need
- 1½ litre (2½ pint) mould

1. In a heavy-based pan, gently heat sugar with 600ml (1 pint) water until sugar dissolves. Increase the heat and boil rapidly for five minutes.

2. Reduce heat and add cranberries to syrup, reserving a few for decoration. Cook for 10–15 minutes until cranberries have popped and are soft and mushy. Remove from heat and add orange and lemon juice. Allow to cool slightly and blitz in a food processor to a purée consistency.

3. Dissolve the gelatine fully in five tablespoons of hot water and then stir into the cranberry mixture. Transfer into a large mixing bowl and allow to cool fully.

4. Whip cream until it forms soft peaks, then fold into the cranberry mixture.

5. Pour into mould and refrigerate until set. Turn out onto serving plate, decorate with the reserved cranberries and serve.

Blessing for the New Year

May the New Year bring
The wealth of home and hearth to you,
The cheer and goodwill of friends to you,
The hope of a childlike heart to you,
The joy of a thousand angels to you,
The love of the Son and God's peace to you.

– Author unknown

“May the saddest day of your future be no worse
Than the happiest day of your past.”

– Irish blessing

King's Pancake

LOUIE CLEMENT, WEXFORD

*In France, where I am from, this cake is eaten on 6 January to celebrate Epiphany Day
or Little Christmas. A trinket is hidden in the cake and whoever finds it in
their slice becomes the King (or Queen) for the day and enjoys such
privileges as having their tea made for them.*

Serves 6–8

- 1 packet of ready-made puff pastry
- 125g (4½oz) ground almonds
- 125g (4½oz) soft butter
- 125g (4½oz) sugar
- 2 large eggs, lightly beaten
- 1½ tablespoons dark rum
- 1–2 tablespoons milk

what you'll need

- small ceramic trinket (optional)
- 24cm (9½in) tart tin with removable base
- pastry brush

1. Preheat oven to 200°C/400°F/Gas 6. Butter and flour the tart tin.

2. Cut pastry in half, roll out on a lightly floured surface and cut a circle large enough to cover the bottom and sides of the tart tin. Line the tin with pastry, trimming away any excess. Pierce pastry base with a fork. Roll the remaining pastry into a second circle to serve as the top of the 'pancake'. Set aside.

3. In a large mixing bowl, mix together the ground almonds, butter, sugar, eggs and rum. Add the ceramic trinket, if using.

4. Brush edges of tart base with a pastry brush dipped in a little milk. Pour the almond mixture over the pastry base and add the top layer of pastry, pressing the edges to seal. Pierce a small hole in the top to allow air to escape during cooking, and score to decorate if you like.

5. Brush the pastry lid with the remaining milk and bake in preheated oven for 30 minutes. Allow to cool a little before removing carefully from tin. Serve warm.

from The Dead

It had begun to snow again. He watched sleepily the flakes, silver and dark, falling obliquely against the landscape. Yes, the newspapers were right: snow was general all over Ireland. It was falling softly upon the Bog of Allen and, further westwards, softly falling into the dark mutinous Shannon waves. It was falling too upon every part of the lonely churchyard where Michael Furey lay buried. It lay thickly drifted on the crooked crosses and headstones, on the spears of the little gate, on the barren thorns. His soul swooned slowly as he heard the snow falling faintly through the universe and faintly falling, like the descent of their last end, upon all the living and the dead.

– James Joyce

"All things must pass."

– Proverb

thank yOu 4
the days

Chapter 8
Simpler Days

"Breakfast like a king,
lunch like a prince and dine like a pauper."
– Proverb

We used to live lives that were shaped and guided by a binding connection with the land and the rhythms of nature. We rose with the dawn to meet the day and withdrew to the fireside with the fall of night. For the longer days of summer, busy, hard-working days of physical labour, we needed to fuel our energy from the start. The traditional Irish fry is indeed a breakfast for kings, and dinner would be taken in the middle of the day. That left the lightest meal of the day to the evening; 'teatime' meals were often simple suppers of hot tea, cold cuts of meat, fish or cheese and some brown bread warmed over the fire, or perhaps potato cakes fried on a skillet pan in the hearth.

❝I believe that a simple and unassuming manner of life is best for everyone, best for both the body and the mind. ❞

– Albert Einstein

Today, things are less straightforward, and how we live our lives often strains against the natural tides of nature. We skip breakfast, fuelling ourselves with coffee instead. We grab a take-away lunch if we are lucky and finally eat our main meal at the end of a long day. But we would do well to remember that simplicity has its own rewards. Sometimes the humblest of meals offers great satisfaction, especially when prepared with love and when shared with the right company and conversation. Being kind to ourselves is not the same as spoiling ourselves; it can be the opposite.

**❝Kindness in words creates confidence.
Kindness in thinking creates profoundness.
Kindness in giving creates love.❞**

– Lao-Tzu

"As a child in the 1940s, being taken for a pie on fair day was an unforgettable event. The traditional West Kerry mutton pie was eaten only on rare and special occasions, such as pattern and fair days, and was a treat for the country people who had travelled to the town by horse and cart or bicycle.

In those days there were no such things as restaurants in country towns to provide sustenance to the locals and visitors. Instead, women would open their homes in the heart of the action, such as those who lived in the small houses on Pie Lane, Tralee. I can remember two old ladies wearing cotton bibs who kept their black pots of soup warm by a blazing turf fire. The pies would be reheated to order in this broth.

Today, mutton pies continue to be made for the few fair days and pattern days that are still celebrated. "

– Mary Fitzgerald, Kerry

Mutton Pies

MARY FITZGERALD, KERRY

This very traditional recipe is part of our Irish heritage. Mutton pies are similar to meat pasties, being pastry-wrapped parcels of meat designed to be eaten as food on the go, but they are traditionally reheated in hot broth before serving.

Makes 12 pies
- 1kg (2½lb) diced lamb, cut into 1cm cubes
- salt and freshly ground black pepper

for the pastry
- 675g (1½lb) self-raising flour, plus extra for dusting
- ½ teaspoon salt
- 85g (3oz) margarine
- 150ml (¼ pint) milk, approximately

for the broth
- lamb or beef bones (ask your butcher for these)
- salt and freshly ground black pepper
- 2 onions, peeled and quartered
- 1 carrot, scrubbed or peeled and roughly chopped
- 1–2 handfuls chopped bacon (optional)

what you'll need
- 6cm (2½in) scone cutter
- baking tray or sheet
- wire rack

1. Preheat oven to 200°C/400°F/Gas 6. Lightly grease and dust a baking tray or sheet. Dice the meat and season well with salt and pepper. Set aside.

2. In a large mixing bowl, add the salt to the flour and rub the margarine into the flour until it resembles breadcrumbs. Add just enough milk to bind together into a stiff dough, reserving a little for sealing the pastry later. You're aiming for a dry pastry as you want it to hold together well in the broth when reheating.

3. On a lightly floured surface, roll out the dough to about 1cm (½in) thickness and cut out rounds with the scone cutter. Roll each round out to a saucer size. Pile the seasoned meat in the middle of half of the pastry rounds, brush the edges with a little milk and top each with another round of pastry, pressing well to seal the edges.

4. Bake in preheated oven for about 25–30 minutes or until nicely browned. Allow to cool fully on a wire rack and then store in an airtight container in the fridge until required.

5. To make the broth, season the bones with salt and pepper, and combine in a large stock pot with onions, carrot and chopped bacon, if using for additional flavour. Cover with water, bring to the boil and then simmer for two hours. Allow to cool fully and strain, skimming off any fat.

6. When ready to serve, bring the required amount of broth to the boil. Pierce a hole in the top of a pie and add to the soup. Simmer for five minutes to reheat and soften the pastry.

ICA Tip
These pies freeze very well, but will also keep for five or six days in the fridge – just make sure they are fully cooled before you refrigerate them.

Spiced Damson Butter

ANN SMITH, DONEGAL

Damson trees can be found in old gardens, where their fruit often goes to waste. This damson butter is like a jelly but is easier to make as, instead of dripping the cooked fruit through a jelly bag for hours, it is pressed through a sieve. This makes it a little less clear, but it is delicious on biscuits with cheese, served with cold meats, terrines or pâté, or stirred into gravies to enrich them.

Makes about 2–3 jars

- 1½kg (3½lb) damsons or plums
- 300ml (10fl oz) water
- 2–3 slices fresh root ginger
- 2 cinnamon sticks, halved
- 2 star anise
- 1kg (2lb) sugar, approximately
- 25g (1oz) butter

what you'll need

- 3 small jam jars
- baking parchment
- string or elastic bands
- labels

1. Halve and stone the damsons and place in a large saucepan. Add the water and spices, and bring to the boil. Simmer for 25–30 minutes or until fruit is pulpy. Meanwhile, pop a saucer in the freezer.

2. Press the pulp through a sieve, pushing as much through as you can, then put it back into the pan, measuring it as you go. Add 500g sugar for each 500ml liquid.

3. Bring to a rolling boil, add the butter and stir until the sugar has fully dissolved. Increase the heat and boil hard for 7–10 minutes or until setting point is reached. Meanwhile, sterilise the jars (see p30 for instructions).

4. To check for setting point, spoon a little onto a very cold saucer. Leave for a minute and then push with your finger. If it wrinkles, it is ready; if it doesn't, return to the boil and cook for a further two or three minutes before testing again.

5. Once the butter has reached setting point, transfer into warm sterilised jars, cover with baking parchment and secure with string or elastic bands. Label with the date and name, and store in a cool dark place.

Chicken Liver Pâté

AN GRIANÁN, LOUTH

There was a time when we wasted as little as possible of whatever food was available to us, and chicken liver pâté was an extra treat that would come with the luxury of killing and roasting a chicken. It keeps well – even better if potted with a butter seal.

Serves 4–6 as part of a light meal

- 200g (7oz) butter
- 2 shallots, chopped
- 1 teaspoon thyme leaves, finely chopped
- 1 clove garlic, finely chopped
- 400g (14oz) chicken livers, cleaned, trimmed and cut in half
- 1–2 tablespoons brandy or Madeira wine
- ¼ teaspoon mustard powder or ground ginger
- salt and freshly ground black pepper
- 80ml (3fl oz) double cream (optional)

to serve
- toasted bread

1. Melt half the butter in a pan over a medium heat, and gently fry the shallots until softened but not coloured.

2. Add the thyme, garlic and chicken livers, and fry the livers until golden brown. Add the brandy or Madeira wine, and the mustard powder or ginger, and season generously with salt and freshly ground black pepper.

3. Place the liver mixture together with half of the remaining butter and the cream, if using, into a food processor and blitz until smooth. Re-season, to taste.

4. Transfer into a serving ramekin or serving dish and chill for 30 minutes. Melt the remaining butter and pour over the pâté before returning it to the fridge to set the butter.

The following is a poem my children learned in Junior Infants:

My mammy was the first person that I ever met
And is the nicest by far that I have seen yet.
She has nice wavy hair and the softest of hands
And whatever I do Mammy quite understands.
It was my daddy who found her, just where I cannot tell,
But one thing is sure: he chose very well.
And I know one thing is certain, she loves me a lot
For she always says I am the nicest girl she has got.

A mother is she who can take the place of all others but whose place no one else can take.

– Therese Pettit, Wexford

66A bell is no bell till you ring it,
A song is no song till you sing it,
And love in your hearts wasn't put there to stay –
Love isn't love till you give it away.**99**

– Oscar Hammerstein

from Any Woman

I am the fire upon the hearth,
I am the light of the good sun,
I am the heat that warms the earth,
Which else were colder than a stone.

At me the children warm their hands;
I am their light of love alive.

– Katharine Tynan

Cauliflower, Ham & Cheese Bake

THERESE PETTIT, WEXFORD

I used to feed this to my children when they came in hungry from school. It was nutritious enough to keep me happy and delicious enough to keep them happy, and is quick and easy to prepare – just what you want in a simple teatime dish.

Serves 4 as a light meal
- 1 large cauliflower
- 50g (2oz) butter
- 25g (1oz) plain flour
- 400ml (¾ pint) milk, warmed
- 150g (5oz) cooked ham, diced
- 150g (5oz) Irish cheddar, grated
- salt and freshly ground black pepper
- 2 handfuls breadcrumbs

what you'll need
- ovenproof casserole dish

1. Preheat oven to 200°C/400°F/Gas 6.

2. Break the cauliflower into florets, pop into a large pot with some salt and set aside. Melt the butter in a large saucepan, stir in the flour and cook together for a few minutes, continuing to stir.

3. Slowly whisk warmed milk into flour mixture and cook gently over a medium to low heat for 10 minutes. Meanwhile, add a kettleful of boiling water to the cauliflower and simmer until just tender. Drain and set aside.

4. Add the ham and cheese to the white sauce, season with salt and pepper, and stir in the cauliflower. Transfer the mixture into a large casserole dish, sprinkle breadcrumbs across the top and bake in preheated oven for 15 minutes or until golden brown and heated through.

Salmon Mousse

LOUIE CLEMENT, WEXFORD

This simple mousse makes a great go-to for when you have friends over for a very casual bite, when it could be served alongside salads and other pâtés. It would also work well as part of a summer picnic.

Serves 6 for a light meal
- 3 tins red salmon (about 500–600g/18–21oz), drained
- 1 small tin tomato purée
- 250ml (8fl oz) crème fraîche (or double cream)
- 200ml (7fl oz) mayonnaise
- 1 lemon, juice and some zest
- salt and freshly ground black pepper

to set the mousse
- 1 sachet of gelatine (about 12g/²⁄₅ oz)
- 250ml (8fl oz) water

to serve
- hot toast
- wedges of lemon

1. Heat the 250ml (8fl oz) water in a small saucepan and add the gelatine. Bring to the boil, then take off the heat and set aside to cool for a few minutes.

2. In a blender or using a fork (depending on the consistency you want to aim for), blitz or mash the salmon, tomato purée, crème fraîche, mayonnaise, lemon juice and a little zest.

3. Add the gelatine water to the salmon mixture and stir thoroughly. Season to taste, adding a little more lemon zest if required.

4. Transfer to a large serving dish, cover loosely with tin foil and refrigerate for several hours or preferably overnight to allow the flavours to develop.

5. Serve on toast or freshly made bread with a couple of wedges of fresh lemon on the side.

Sardine Eggs

RITA HORGAN, LIMERICK

This recipe is based on a 1940s press cutting in my mother's scrapbook, which I have treasured since her untimely death in 1966. My mother loved plain wholesome cooking and I can still recall the welcome aroma of her freshly baked scones and tarts, and her delicious stuffed pork steak, roast beef and Yorkshire pudding.

Serves 4 for a light meal
- 4 eggs
- 6 sardines (tinned or cooked)
- 1–2 teaspoons chopped parsley
- 25g (1oz) margarine
- dash of lemon juice or vinegar, to taste
- anchovy essence or umami paste, to taste (optional)
- salt and freshly ground black pepper

for the homemade mayonnaise (optional)
- 2 egg yolks
- 1 tablespoon Dijon mustard
- salt and freshly ground black pepper
- 275ml (½ pint) sunflower or olive oil
- white wine vinegar or lemon juice, to taste

to serve
- mayonnaise (shop bought or as per recipe above)
- fresh lettuce
- slices of cucumber

1. If you're making your own mayonnaise, whisk two egg yolks together with mustard and season well. Drizzle in the oil very slowly, continuing to whisk. Once the yolks and oil begin to emulsify, you can add the oil in faster. Finish with a little vinegar or lemon juice to taste and refrigerate until needed (use within a week).

2. Hard boil the four eggs. One method is to cover the eggs in cold salted water in a medium saucepan, bring to the boil and reduce to a simmer for one minute. Then cover and remove from heat, and set aside to cook for 10–12 minutes.

3. Meanwhile, bone the sardines and scrape the flesh into a small bowl.

4. To peel the eggs, run them under cold water to make them cool enough to handle, then crack a circle around the widest part of the egg. Twist the two halves gently and ease the shell away, peeling away any remaining pieces.

5. Halve each egg, remove the yolks and set the whites aside. Add the yolks to the sardines and mash together. Add the parsley and margarine, and mix well. Season to taste with lemon juice, a little anchovy essence or umami paste (if using), pepper and salt – in that order and tasting as you go.

6. Fill the whites of the eggs with this mixture, arrange on salad leaves scattered with cucumber slices and serve with mayonnaise.

from Digging

Under my window, a clean rasping sound
When the spade sinks into gravelly ground:
My father, digging.

...

The coarse boot nestled on the lug, the shaft
Against the inside knee was levered firmly.
He rooted out tall tops, buried the bright edge deep
To scatter new potatoes that we picked,
Loving their cool hardness in our hands.

By God, the old man could handle a spade.
Just like his old man.

...

But I've no spade to follow men like them.

Between my finger and my thumb
The squat pen rests.
I'll dig with it.

– Seamus Heaney

**"There's virtue in the soil
That has been turned by countless spades,
And in earth's heart a seed is dropped
By every flower that fades."**

– Kathleen Partridge

**"If you want to go fast, go alone;
if you want to go far, go together."**

– African proverb

Potato Cakes

ANNE PAYNE, LAOIS

Leftover potatoes can be used as a base for many a simple teatime meal. They can be transformed into potato cakes and served with anything from black pudding and apple sauce to smoked fish and sour cream, or hot crispy bacon and grilled tomato.

Makes 9 potato cakes

- 450g (1lb) potatoes, peeled, cooked and mashed
- 50g (2oz) plain flour, plus extra for shaping
- 1 egg, beaten
- 3 scallions (spring onions), finely chopped
- salt and freshly ground black pepper
- a little milk
- oil, for frying
- generous knob of butter (optional)

1. Combine the potato, flour, egg and scallions in a mixing bowl and season with salt and pepper. Mix well until all ingredients come together. You may need to add a little milk if the mixture is too dry, but don't make the consistency too loose or sticky.

2. Using a small amount of flour to dust your hands each time, shape the mixture into nine small potato cakes.

3. Heat oil in a pan together with butter, if using, and cook the potato cakes over a medium heat until heated through and nicely browned on each side (about three to four minutes each side).

4. Cakes can be served immediately or kept overnight in a fridge and reheated in a hot oven (200°C/400°F/Gas 6) for about 15 minutes before serving.

During my grandmother's and great-grandmother's time, life was very difficult for most women here in Ireland. There was no running water. Wells were often a considerable distance away from the dwelling house. Imagine carrying buckets of water to the kitchen before starting to wash babies or their nappies. Imagine keeping the open fire going for boiling water, cooking or baking bread. It was like a form of slavery or drudgery.

When young people today experiment with outdoor activities like lighting fires and cooking outdoors, it really is great fun. Just watch the Scouts and Guides.

When I think of the last few centuries of Irish women trying to light a fire with damp turf or poor quality coal, I marvel at how the modern woman has instant heat at the flick of a switch. She can even talk to her computer and it will do the typing for her. In this age of Skype and FaceTime and affordable flights, no wonder our grandchildren can't comprehend why families went to faraway places like America or Australia and never came home again. How hard the American wake must have been on the poor parents who saw their children disappear one by one.

Our grandchildren live in such an exciting era. The smallest child is an expert on all types of phones and computers, tablets and PlayStations. We have a duty to help the modern child to recognise the wonderful world we now live in and also to help them appreciate all things bright and beautiful, all creatures great and small, all things wise and wonderful – the Lord God made them all.

– Eva Coyle, Donegal

Leitrim Boxty

NORA RYAN, SLIGO

Boxty is particular to a few counties in the north-east of the country; this recipe is something of a purist version common to lovely County Leitrim. It is particularly nice reheated in a pan that has just been used to fry some rashers.

Serves 4

- 4 large raw potatoes, peeled
- 1 egg, beaten
- 200g (7oz) plain flour
- 150ml (¼ pint) milk, or as required
- 1 teaspoon bicarbonate of soda
- pinch of salt (optional)
- oil, for frying
- generous knob of butter (optional)

1. Grate potatoes into a large mixing bowl and add beaten egg. Little by little, add enough flour and milk as required to bind the mix and bring it to the dropping consistency of a thick pancake batter. Add the soda and salt, and mix well.

2. Heat a little oil in a pan together with butter, if using. Pour or spoon in about one eighth of the mixture and cook as you would a pancake, gently frying each boxty cake over a medium heat until cooked through and nicely browned (about six to eight minutes on each side). Remove from the pan and keep warm while you repeat with the rest of the mixture. There should be enough for about eight cakes.

3. These can be served immediately or stored in an airtight container and reheated on a hot pan until warmed sufficiently.

66 May you be blessed with
Warmth in your home,
Love in your heart,
Peace in your soul,
And joy in your life. **99**

– Irish blessing

---

66 Love is patient and kind; love is not jealous or boastful;
it is not arrogant or rude.
It does not insist on its own way; it is not irritable or resentful;
it does not rejoice in wrongdoing, but rejoices in the truth.
It bears all things, believes all things, hopes all things, endures all things. **99**

– 1 Corinthians 13:4–8

---

66 Health and long life to you!
Land without rent to you!
A child every year to you!
And may you die in Ireland. **99**

– Irish toast

♡

KINDNESS
IN
GIVING
CREATES

Love!

Appendices

Useful Equipment & Glossary
Contributors
Acknowledgements
Sources

Useful Equipment & Glossary

A FEW WORDS ABOUT TEMPERATURES AND MEASUREMENTS

Please note that, as with our *Irish Countrywomen's Association Cookbook*, all temperatures given throughout this book are for conventional ovens. If you have a fan oven, reduce the suggested temperature by about 20°C (e.g. from 200°C to 180°C).

Note that all teaspoon measurements are for a level teaspoon, unless otherwise specified. All tablespoon measurements are for a level tablespoon, and not for a dessertspoon unless otherwise specified.

Both metric and imperial measurements have been provided. It is best to follow one or the other, as in some cases they have been rounded up or down for the purpose of the recipe, e.g. 1oz is equal to 28g, but the latter has been rounded down to 25g.

Useful Equipment

Baking beans: these dried uncooked beans are used to weigh down pastry while baking blind (see glossary); the beans can be retained after baking for re-use.

Baking parchment: also known as silicone paper, baking paper or greaseproof paper, this is essential for many baking recipes in order to line baking tins; also useful for sealing jars of homemade preserves.

Baking sheet: a flat baking sheet (as opposed to a shallow baking tray) is very useful for baking certain breads and cakes, and can be preheated for optimum results.

Blender: a stand-alone electrical appliance used for chopping, mixing or liquidising foods.

Bun tin: also known as a patty tin, this is a baking tray with six, nine or twelve cup depressions for making buns and mini-pies.

Cake tin: cake tins come in various sizes and shapes. If using a square tin rather than a round one, reduce the dimensions by 2½cm (1in).

Casserole dish: a large ovenproof lidded dish for cooking stews in the oven or on the stove top.

Chopping board: it is good practice to allocate one chopping board to dealing with raw meats and fish, another to vegetables, including pungent onions and garlic, and another to fruits and bread. Always wash in hot soapy water after using for raw meat and fish.

Flan tin: also known as a quiche tin or tart tin, these often have a removable base.

Food processor: a multi-functional appliance that has a container and a number of different removable revolving blades that allow food to be cut, sliced, shredded, blended, beaten or liquidised in the container.

Frying pan: whether you have a modern non-stick frying pan or an old-fashioned cast iron one, the weight of the pan is important; a heavy-based pan distributes heat more evenly and is less likely to burn food.

Grater: a good grater is a real friend in the kitchen; look for one with several grades of fineness or invest in a selection of quality graters.

Hand blender: also known as a billy, a hand-held electrical appliance is useful for liquidising, blending or puréeing foods, such as soups, without having to transfer them from the cooking vessel.

Jam jars: essential for jam making and useful for presenting homemade gifts such as lemon curd, it is worth setting aside a few of these for recycling; see p30 for instructions on sterilising jars.

Labels: essential for keeping track of frozen foods, which should always be clearly labelled with details of content and the date; likewise for homemade preserves.

Loaf tin: tins for bread making are usually defined by the volume they hold rather than their shape (e.g. 900g (2lb) loaf tin).

Loose-bottomed tin: baking tin with removable base that allows the cake to be easily removed.

Measuring jug: plastic, Pyrex or glass jug for measuring liquids; it is worth having both metric and imperial measurements on this, as well as American cups.

Measuring spoons: stainless-steel collection of spoons, including teaspoons and tablespoons.

Melon baller: useful for balling melon or potatoes and for coring apples and pears.

Mixer: a stand-alone appliance with interchangeable blades; useful for everything from folding and whipping to beating and mixing ingredients.

Muffin tin: similar to a bun tin but deeper.

Pastry brush: choose a silicone one, which is easy to wash.

Peeler: life is too short to use a bad peeler. There are various versions out there, so experiment.

Ramekin: individual round ceramic dishes useful for making various pies and puddings.

Rolling pin: a good rolling pin is essential for baking with pastry; some like to use a ceramic one to keep the pastry extra cool.

Scone cutter: also known as a pastry cutter or a cookie cutter. It is useful to have cutters in a variety of sizes for use in all sorts of baking. However, if stuck without one, a smooth-rimmed glass can be used in its place.

Sieve: it is worth having a general sieve for use with dry ingredients when baking, as well as a colander (for draining wet ingredients) and perhaps a fine chinois for passing purées.

Skewers: to judge whether cakes and baked goods are fully cooked, a metal skewer can be inserted into the centre; if the skewer comes out clean, your cake is ready.

Spring-form cake tin: a cake tin with detachable bottom and collar to facilitate removal of delicate desserts and cakes.

Thermometer: sugar or jam thermometers may be worth investing in if you plan on making a lot of jam. A meat thermometer is useful to judge the central temperature of a large joint of meat.

Weighing scales: if you like to bake, an electronic scales might be worth investing in, as it allows you to measure very refined and exact weights.

Wire rack: this is essential for baking, generating the necessary circulation of air for forming a good crust on bread and for cooling cakes.

Glossary

Bain-marie: a system for cooking something in a container such as a bowl, where the container is set over boiling water to ensure a gentle cooking process.

Bake blind: to bake a pastry base prior to filling, in order to ensure a crisp rather than a soggy base. The base is lined with baking parchment and weighed down with dried baking beans so its shape is maintained.

Bicarbonate of soda: also known as sodium bicarbonate, bread soda or baking soda, this differs from baking powder and requires an acid such as buttermilk to activate its leavening properties.

Bind: to moisten and bring together dry ingredients with a small amount of liquid in order to form into a paste or dough.

Blanch: a technique for par-cooking vegetables. Boiling briefly and then arresting the cooking and placing the vegetables in cold or iced water helps retain a firm texture and bright colour.

Blitz: to blend to a purée with a hand blender or in a blender.

Cook's knife: a good, well-maintained knife will do much to improve your cooking; always store carefully to keep it as sharp as possible.

Crimp: a term for impressing a patterned seal on a pastry rim; this can be done with fingers, a fork or a knife.

Fillet: if buying whole fish, you can ask your fishmonger to prepare it by gutting, removing the head and removing the fish fillets from the bones.

Fold: in baking, the gentle action of folding incorporates dry ingredients such as flour or sugar into whipped ingredients such as whipped egg white or cream, while retaining as much air as possible in the whipped ingredients.

Low-GI: the term GI refers to Glycemic Index, which measures the relationship between carbohydrates consumed and resulting blood-sugar levels. Low-GI foods release glucose more slowly and steadily.

Pin boning: some fillets of fish will still have large pin bones running down along the side; check for these with your fingers and remove with a large flat tweezers.

Sauté: to fry vegetables such as onion very quickly in order to brown and caramelise while cooking; do not stir too often.

Sear: also known as browning, this is cooking meat quickly on a high heat in order to encourage caramelisation of sugars.

Sweat: to fry vegetables such as onion very slowly and gently in order to soften without browning; it helps to cover the pan with a lid and perhaps some greaseproof paper to keep the moisture in.

Toast: nuts, seeds and spices can be toasted on a dry frying pan, under a hot grill or in a low oven in order to release aromas; watch closely to make sure they don't burn.

Contributors

The ICA would like to thank all the Guilds and individual members who opened up their scrapbooks, notebooks and recipe collections to share their tried and tested recipes and beloved words of reflection with us all.

An Grianán, Louth
Angela Galvin, Cork
Ann O'Connor, Wexford
Ann Smith, Donegal
Anna Sinnott, Wicklow
Anne Carleton, Cork
Anne Kearins, Sligo
Anne Payne, Laois
Beltra Guild Members, Sligo
Betty Gorman, Laois
Breda Brown, Kerry
Breda McDonald, Kilkenny
Breege Haugh, Mayo
Bríd Fitzpatrick, Kilkenny
Bridget Withero, Tipperary
Bridie Kelly Doyle, Wexford
Carmel Dawson, Carlow
Caroline Power, Meath
Catherine O'Neill, Wexford
Connie McEvoy, Louth
Edward Hayden, ICA cookery tutor
Eileen McGlew, Louth
Eileen Sheehan, Cork
Eithne Lee, Wexford
Elizabeth Murphy, Laois
Emily McCarthy, Dublin
Emily Murphy, Wexford
Eva Coyle, Donegal
Imelda O'Connor, Cork
Iris Farrell, Louth
Jane Johnston, Longford
Josephine Keane, Wexford
Josephine O'Reilly, Wexford

June Lawless, Dublin
Kathleen Tessyman, Cork
Kay Murray, Clare
Liz Wall, Wicklow
Louie Clement, Wexford
Mamo McDonald, Monaghan
Margaret Bowkett, Wexford
Margaret Sides, Longford
Mary Fitzgerald, Kerry
Mary Fitzgerald, Wexford
Mary M. Spillane, Kerry
Mary McNamara, Kildare
Mary O'Reilly, Mayo
Maura Davis, Wicklow
Maura Mohan, Monaghan
Maura Riordan, Dublin
Muriel Kerr, Leitrim
Nellie Dillon, Kildare
Nora Ryan, Sligo
Norah Clifford-Kelly, Wexford
Pat Lynch, Cork
Pat Moran, Dublin
Patricia Cavanagh, Monaghan
Peg Prendeville, Limerick
Peggy Quinn, Meath
Phil Kiernan, Westmeath
Rita Horgan, Limerick
Rosemary McCarville, Monaghan
Sally Dunleavy, Mayo
Teresa Dooner, Longford
Therese Pettit, Wexford
Winnie McCarron, Monaghan
Yvonne Kelly, Tipperary

Acknowledgements

Liz Wall, National President of the Irish Countrywomen's Association, would like to thank the following people for their help with putting together this special collection of recipes and reflections for every day:

There are always many people to thank for a collaborative work of this nature and as with our two previous books I would most of all like to thank the wonderful members of the ICA. Their skills are varied and numerous, and without their input we wouldn't have any books and certainly not of this calibre.

I would also like to thank **Joanne Dunne** in ICA Central Office for her administrative work in collating all the submissions;

Edward Hayden for his attention to detail in trouble-shooting recipes;

Photographer **Joanne Murphy**, stylists **Carly** and **Blondie Horan** and designer **Tanya Ross** for capturing so beautifully the spirit of the reflections and the deliciousness of the recipes in this book;

And finally, all the team at Gill & Macmillan for having the vision for this unique book and for seeing it through so professionally.

Sources

The publisher and editor would like to thank the following for their kind permission to reproduce copyrighted extracts within this publication:

Extracts "Nothing wastes more energy than worrying," (p31) and "...Count your blessings, not your troubles," (p63) are from the poem '24 Things to Always Remember... and One Thing to Never Forget' by Douglas Pagels. Copyright © 2002 by Blue Mountain Arts, Inc. Reprinted by permission. All rights reserved.

Extract (p38) from poem 'Bread' from *Familiar Strangers: New & Selected Poems 1960–2004* (Bloodaxe Books, 2004) by Brendan Kennelly reprinted with kind permission of publishers.

'A Friendship Blessing' from *Anam Cara* by John O'Donohue, published by Vintage. Reprinted (p68) by kind permission of The Random House Group Limited.

Extract (p81) from poem 'Begin' from *Familiar Strangers: New & Selected Poems 1960–2004* (Bloodaxe Books, 2004) by Brendan Kennelly reprinted with kind permission of publishers.

Extract (p136) from 'A Burren Prayer', from *Conamara Blues* by John O'Donohue, published by Vintage. Reprinted by kind permission of The Random House Group Limited.

Extract "When fruit has ripened on the tree" (p149) from *The Friendship Book of Francis Gay 1983*, by Francis Gay, reprinted by kind permission of © DC Thomson & Co. Ltd. 2014.

Extract (p180) from poem 'Digging' from *Opened Ground* by Seamus Heaney reprinted with kind permission of Faber and Faber Ltd.

The publisher and editor have made every effort to trace all copyright holders, but if any has been inadvertently overlooked we would be pleased to make the necessary arrangement at the first opportunity.

Index

A

adages 20, 27, 34, 52, 59, 81
Alcott, Louisa May 93
Ali, Muhammad 49
All-Bran, Iced Raisin Bars 15
almonds
    Almond Biscuits 123
    Almond Paste 146
    Almond Tartlets 89
    Chocolate Florentines **66**, 67
    Cut-before-Christmas Cranberry Cake 155
    Flour-free Fruit Cake 60, **61**
    Gâteau Flamand **86**, 87
    King's Pancake 160, **161**
    Moist Almond Slices 111
    Simnel Cake **144**, 145
Any Woman (Tynan) 173
apples
    Apple and Rhubarb Pie 62
    Mid-Western Apple Cake 150, **151**
    Toffee Apple Muffins **8**, 9

B

bain-marie 193
Baked Cherry Cheesecake 109
baking
    baking blind 193
    bicarbonate of soda 193
    equipment 190–91
    folding 193
    pastry crimping 193
Barnes, Emilie 122
bars
    Iced Raisin Bars 15
    Orange Chocolate Bars **16**, 17
Battenberg Cake **44**, 45
Beatitudes for Friends of the Aged (Walker) 85
Beltra Guild Members
    Battenberg Cake **44**, 45
    Chocolate Swiss Roll **56**, 57
    Gingerbread 103
    Marmalade Shortcakes 64, **65**
    Milk Rolls 39
    Queen Cakes 12, **13**
    Rock Cakes 11

bereavement 51, 59
biscuits
    Almond Biscuits 123
    Marmalade Shortcakes 64, **65**
blessings 71, 73, 75, 102, 158, 186
    Beatitudes for Friends of the Aged (Walker) 85
    Blessing for the New Year 158
    Christmas Tree Blessing 154
    Friendship Blessing, A (O'Donohue) 68
    Washing-up Blessing 18
    see also prayers
Bowkett, Margaret 40
    Drop Scones 41
boxty, Leitrim Boxty 185
brack, Tea Brack **120**, 121
bread
    Guinness Bread 37
    Iris's Idiot-proof Brown Bread 32
    Milk Rolls 39
    Wheat-free Brown Bread 33
    see also scones
Bread (Kennelly) 38
Brown, Breda 154
    Cut-before-Christmas Cranberry Cake 155
    Lemon Cake 128
Brown, Les 10
buns, Orange and Cinnamon Hot Cross Buns 143
Burren Prayer, A (O'Donohue) 136
Butterfly Cakes 12, **13**

C

cake tins 190, 191
cakes
    Battenberg Cake **44**, 45
    Cathryn's Crazy Chocolate Bake 80
    Chocolate Swiss Roll **56**, 57
    Coffee Ring Cake 58
    Courgette Cake 100, **101**
    Dutch Rhubarb Cake 97
    Flour-free Fruit Cake 60, **61**
    Gingerbread 103
    Honey Spice Cake 104, **105**
    Lemon Cake 128
    Mid-Western Apple Cake 150, **151**

Mother's Malt Cake Loaf **76**, 77

Nora De Buitléar's Special Occasion
    Dream Cake 78, **79**

Queen Cakes 12, **13**

Rich-in-Love Chocolate Cake 53

Rock Cakes 11

see also bars; biscuits; cheesecakes;
    desserts; muffins; pastry

Campbell, Joseph 90

Carleton, Anne 31

Carrigy, Aoife xi

Carroll, Lewis 10

Carrot, Cranberry and Seed Muffins 6, **7**

Cathryn's Crazy Chocolate Bake 80

Cauliflower, Ham and Cheese Bake 174, **175**

Cheat's Passion Fruit and Lime Soufflé 133

cheese

    Baked Cherry Cheesecake 109

    Cauliflower, Ham and Cheese Bake 174,
        175

    Curd Cheesecake 110

    Mango Cheesecake 134, **135**

    Quarkblätterteig 124, **125**

cheesecakes

    Baked Cherry Cheesecake 109

    Curd Cheesecake 110

    Mango Cheesecake 134, **135**

Chekhov, Anton 117

cherries, Baked Cherry Cheesecake 109

Chicken Liver Pâté 172

chocolate

    Chocolate Florentines **66**, 67

    Chocolate Swiss Roll **56**, 57

    Crunchy Chocolate Meringue Cake 84

    Maltesers Rocky Road 19

    Nora De Buitléar's Special Occasion
        Dream Cake 78, **79**

    Orange Chocolate Bars **16**, 17

    Rich-in-Love Chocolate Cake 53

chopping boards 190

Christmas 140

    Cranberry Mousse **156**, 157

    Cut-before-Christmas Cranberry Cake
        155

Christmas Tree Blessing 154

Citrus Poppy Seed Cake **130**, 131

Clement, Louie

    King's Pancake 160, **161**

    Salmon Mousse **176**, 177

Climbing Boots 106

coeliacs

    Almond Tartlets 89

    Flour-free Fruit Cake 60, **61**

Coffee Ring Cake 58

Cohen, Leonard 20

cooking

    equipment 190–91

    measurements 190

    oven temperatures 190

    terminology 193

Corinthians 13:4–8 186

cottage cheese

    Baked Cherry Cheesecake 109

    Curd Cheesecake 110

    Quarkblätterteig 124, **125**

Courgette Cake 100, **101**

Coyle, Eva 184

cranberries

    Carrot, Cranberry and Seed Muffins 6, **7**

    Cranberry Mousse **156**, 157

    Cut-before-Christmas Cranberry Cake
        155

cream cheese

    icings 100, 131

    Mango Cheesecake 134, **135**

Cronin, Anthony J. 18, 63

Crunchy Chocolate Meringue Cake 84

Curd Cheesecake 110

custard

    Cheat's Passion Fruit and Lime Soufflé 133

    Homemade Custard 147

Cut-before-Christmas Cranberry Cake 155

D

Daffodils, The (Wordsworth) 112

Dalí, Salvador 3

damsons, Spiced Damson Butter 170

Davies, W.H. 31

De Buitléar, Nora 78

Dead, The (Joyce) 162

desserts

    Cheat's Passion Fruit and Lime Soufflé 133

    Cranberry Mousse **156**, 157

Digging (Heaney) 180
Dillon, Nellie, Chocolate Florentines **66**, 67
Dooner, Teresa, Tea Brack **120**, 121
dried fruit
    Carrot, Cranberry and Seed Muffins 6, **7**
    Cut-before-Christmas Cranberry Cake
        155
    Flour-free Fruit Cake 60, **61**
    Iced Raisin Bars 15
    Mother's Malt Cake Loaf **76**, 77
    Nora De Buitléar's Special Occasion
        Dream Cake 78, **79**
    Orange and Cinnamon Hot Cross Buns
        143
    Queen Cakes 12
    Rock Cakes 11
    Simnel Cake **144**, 145
    Tea Brack **120**, 121
Drop Scones 40, 41
Dunleavy, Peg 127
Dunleavy, Sally 59
    Lemon Curd **126**, 127
Dutch Rhubarb Cake 97

E

Earhart, Amelia 63
Easter 140, 142
    Orange and Cinnamon Hot Cross Buns
        143
    Simnel Cake **144**, 145
Einstein, Albert 166
Epiphany Day 160

F

Farrell, Iris, Iris's Idiot-proof Brown Bread 32
festivals/feast days 140
Fields, Dorothy 52, 98
fish
    filleting 193
    pin boning 193
    Salmon Mousse **176**, 177
    Sardine Eggs 179
Fitzgerald, F. Scott 102
Fitzgerald, Mary (Kerry) 168
    Mutton Pies 169
Fitzgerald, Mary (Wexford)
    Iced Raisin Bars 15
    Mid-Western Apple Cake 150, **151**

Fleming, Gerald 96
Flour-free Fruit Cake 60, **61**
Fosdick, Harry Emerson 106
friendship 49, 51, 68, 122, 129
Friendship Blessing, A (O'Donohue) 68

G

Gandhi, Mahatma 1
Gâteau Flamand **86**, 87
Gay, Francis 149
generosity 122
Gibran, Kahlil 18, 122
Gingerbread 103
gluten-free cakes
    Almond Tartlets 89
    Flour-free Fruit Cake 60, **61**
God's Phone Number 59
Gorman, Betty, Almond Biscuits 123
gratitude 63
Grianán, An
    Apple and Rhubarb Pie 62
    Cheat's Passion Fruit and Lime Soufflé 133
    Chicken Liver Pâté 172
    Citrus Poppy Seed Cake **130**, 131
    Homemade Custard 147
    Mango Cheesecake 134, **135**
    Wheat-free Brown Bread 33
Guinness Bread 37

H

Halloween 140, 152, 153
ham, Cauliflower, Ham and Cheese Bake 174, **175**
Hammerstein, Oscar 173
happiness 98, 117, 129
Hardinge, Frances 25
harvest time 149, 150
Hayden, Edward
    Almond Paste 146
    Orange and Cinnamon Hot Cross Buns
        143
    Raspberry Jam 30
    Scones with Raspberry Jam **28**, 29
hazelnuts, Crunchy Chocolate Meringue Cake
    84
Heaney, Seamus 180
Hepburn, Audrey 85
Hesselden, Iris 5

Homemade Custard 147
Honey Spice Cake 104, **105**
Horgan, Rita, Sardine Eggs 179
hospitality 122
Hot Cross Buns 143
Hugo, Victor 102

I

I love a house that's lived in 20
ICA cookery tutor *see* Hayden, Edward
ICA motto 3
Iced Raisin Bars 15
icings/fillings
    Almond Paste 146
    chocolate and orange icing 17
    coffee icing 58
    cream cheese and citrus 131
    cream cheese icing 100
    glacé icing 15
    lemon icing 128
    orange and cinnamon glaze 143
    vanilla cream filling 57
In Praise of Tea (Hesselden) 5
Irish proverbs 94, 149
Irish toast 186
Iris's Idiot-proof Brown Bread 32

J

jack-o'-lantern 152
jam
    Lemon Curd **126**, 127
    Raspberry Jam 30
    Spiced Damson Butter 170
    sugar thermometer 191
Joyce, James 162
Just a Little Hug (Matthews) 132

K

Keller, Helen 54
Kennedy, John F. 54
Kennelly, Brendan 38, 81
kindness 166
King's Pancake 160, **161**
Kinks, The 139
Kinnear, Elizabeth 98
kitchen equipment 190–91

L

Lacemaker's Prayer 88
Lake Isle of Innisfree, The (Yeats) 42
Lao-Tzu 46, 162
Latimer, Hugh 136
laughter 75, 85, 102
Ledwidge, Francis 8
Lee, Eithne 88
    Almond Tartlets 89
Leisure (Davies) 31
Leitrim Boxty 185
lemons
    Citrus Poppy Seed Cake **130**, 131
    Lemon Cake 128
    Lemon Curd **126**, 127
    Quarkblätterteig 124, **125**
Lewis, C.S. 23, 27
limes, Cheat's Passion Fruit and Lime Soufflé
    133
Little Christmas 160
liver, Chicken Liver Pâté 172
love 52, 75, 166, 186
low-GI 193
    Carrot, Cranberry and Seed Muffins 6, **7**
Lughnasa 150

M

McCarron, Winnie, Moist Almond Slices 111
McCarthy, Emily 142
McCarville, Rosemary, Mother's Malt Cake Loaf
    76, 77
MacCathmhaoil, Seosamh 90
McDonald, Mamo
    Cathryn's Crazy Chocolate Bake 80
    Nora De Buitléar's Special Occasion
        Dream Cake 78, **79**
Make Some Moments 27
Maltesers Rocky Road 19
Mango Cheesecake 134, **135**
Marmalade Shortcakes 64, **65**
Marx, Groucho 90
marzipan
    Almond Paste 146
    Battenberg Cake **44**, 45
    Simnel Cake **144**, 145
Matthew 5:4 51

Matthews, Emily 132
May Day 140
mayonnaise 179
measurements 190
meitheal 96
memories 73
meringue, Crunchy Chocolate Meringue Cake
    84
Mid-Western Apple Cake 150, **151**
Milk Rolls 39
Mohan, Maura, Maltesers Rocky Road 19
Moist Almond Slices 111
Mother's Malt Cake Loaf **76**, 77
mousses
    Cranberry Mousse **156**, 157
    Salmon Mousse **176**, 177
muffins
    Carrot, Cranberry and Seed Muffins 6, **7**
    Toffee Apple Muffins **8**, 9
Murphy, C.E. 122
Murray, Cormac 96
Murray, Kay 96
    Dutch Rhubarb Cake 97
Mutton Pies 169

N

Niebuhr, Reinhold 31
Night (Prendeville) 34
no-bake cakes
    Cathryn's Crazy Chocolate Bake 80
    Maltesers Rocky Road 19
    Nora De Buitléar's Special Occasion
        Dream Cake 78, **79**
Nora De Buitléar's Special Occasion Dream Cake
    78
nuts
    Cathryn's Crazy Chocolate Bake 80
    Chocolate Florentines **66**, 67
    Crunchy Chocolate Meringue Cake 84
    Mid-Western Apple Cake 150, **151**
    toasting 193
    see also almonds

O

oatmeal, Orange Chocolate Bars **16**, 17
O'Brien, Edna 122
O'Connor, Gisela 124

O'Donohue, John 46, 68, 118, 136
old age 85, 90
Old Woman, The (MacCathmhaoil) 90
oranges
    Citrus Poppy Seed Cake **130**, 131
    Orange Chocolate Bars **16**, 17
    Orange and Cinnamon Hot Cross Buns
        143
oven temperatures 190

P

Pagels, Douglas 31, 63
Partridge, Kathleen 180
passion fruit, Cheat's Passion Fruit and Lime
    Soufflé 133
pastry
    Apple and Rhubarb Pie 62
    Curd Cheesecake 110
    King's Pancake 160, **161**
    Mutton Pies 169
    Pumpkin Pie 153
    Quarkblätterteig 124, **125**
    Summer Fruit Family Slice 82
    sweet pastry 111
pâté, Chicken Liver Pâté 172
Payne, Anne 118
    Potato Cakes **182**, 183
    Simnel Cake **144**, 145
Payne, Roman 94
Pettit, Therese 173
    Cauliflower, Ham and Cheese Bake 174,
        175
pies
    Apple and Rhubarb Pie 62
    Mutton Pies 169
    Pumpkin Pie 153
poems
    Any Woman (Tynan) 173
    Bread (Kennelly) 38
    Climbing Boots 106
    Daffodils, The (Wordsworth) 112
    Digging (Heaney) 180
    God's Phone Number 59
    I love a house that's lived in 20
    In Praise of Tea (Hesselden) 5
    Just a Little Hug (Matthews) 132
    Lake Isle of Innisfree, The (Yeats) 42

Make Some Moments 27
Night (Prendeville) 34
Old Woman, The (MacCathmhaoil) 90
Sounds of Summer (Prendeville) 98
When summer comes with long fine days (Murray) 96
Wind that Shakes the Barley, The (Tynan) 112
Woodcarver, The (Strong) 154
poppy seeds, Citrus Poppy Seed Cake **130**, 131
potatoes
    Leitrim Boxty 185
    Potato Cakes **182**, 183
Power, Caroline 52
    Rich-in-Love Chocolate Cake 53
prayers 10
    Burren Prayer, A (O'Donohue) 136
    God 10
    Lacemaker's Prayer 88
    Serenity Prayer (Niebuhr) 31
    see also blessings
Prendeville, Peg 34, 98
proverbs 5, 106, 115, 162, 165, 180
    Irish proverbs 94, 149
pumpkins 152
    Pumpkin Pie 153

Q
Quarkblätterteig 124, **125**
Queen Cakes 12, **13**

R
rainy days 117–18
raspberries
    Almond Tartlets 89
    Raspberry Jam 30
rhubarb
    Apple and Rhubarb Pie 62
    Dutch Rhubarb Cake 97
Rich-in-Love Chocolate Cake 53
Riordan, Maura 152
    Baked Cherry Cheesecake 109
    Courgette Cake 100, **101**
    Cranberry Mousse **156**, 157
    Guinness Bread 37
    Pumpkin Pie 153
    Quarkblätterteig 124, **125**

Rock Cakes 11
rolls, Milk Rolls 39
Roosevelt, Eleanor 5, 68
Ryan, Nora
    Flour-free Fruit Cake 60, **61**
    Leitrim Boxty 185

S
St Brigid's Day 140
Saki xi
Salmon Mousse **176**, 177
Sardine Eggs 179
sauces
    cheese sauce 174
    chocolate sauce 84
    Homemade Custard 147
    mayonnaise 179
Schuller, Robert 51
scones
    Drop Scones 41
    Dutch Rhubarb Cake 97
    Scones with Raspberry Jam **28**, 29
seeds
    Carrot, Cranberry and Seed Muffins 6, **7**
    Citrus Poppy Seed Cake **130**, 131
    toasting 193
Serenity Prayer (Niebuhr) 31
Shaw, George Bernard 3
shortbread, Marmalade Shortcakes 64, **65**
Sides, Margaret
    Honey Spice Cake 104, **105**
    Orange Chocolate Bars **16**, 17
Simnel Cake **144**, 145
Sinnott, Anna 10
Smith, Ann, Spiced Damson Butter 170
Socrates 25
soufflé, Cheat's Passion Fruit and Lime Soufflé 133
Sounds of Summer (Prendeville) 98
sour milk, making 103
soya margarine 15
soya milk, Wheat-free Brown Bread 33
Spiced Damson Butter 170
Spillane, Mary M., Gâteau Flamand **86**, 87
Stoppard, Tom 85
Strong, Patience 154
Summer Fruit Family Slice 82

Swift, Jonathan 40, 90

T

Tea Brack **120**, 121
Teale, Edwin Way 54
Ten Golden Rules for Every Busy Woman 14
Teresa, Mother 34
Toffee Apple Muffins **8**, 9
Tynan, Katharine 112, 173

U

Urban Shaman (Murphy) 122

V

vegetables
      blanching 193
      sautéing 193
      sweating 193

W

Walker, Esther Mary 85
Wall, Liz x
      Coffee Ring Cake 58
      Crunchy Chocolate Meringue Cake 84
      Curd Cheesecake 110
      Summer Fruit Family Slice 82
      Toffee Apple Muffins **8**, 9
Washing-up Blessing 18
Watch your thoughts 46
West, Mae 149
Wheat-free Brown Bread 33
When things go wrong 54
Wilde, Oscar 25, 142
Wind that Shakes the Barley, The (Tynan) 112
Woodcarver, The (Strong) 154
Wordsworth, William 112

Y

yeast, Orange and Cinnamon Hot Cross Buns
      143
Yeats, W.B. 42, 68
yofu, Wheat-free Brown Bread 33
yoghurt 103
      Citrus Poppy Seed Cake **130**, 131

Notes

Notes

Notes

Notes